Coastal Ecosystems

ECOLOGICAL CONSIDERATIONS FOR MANAGEMENT OF THE COASTAL ZONE

By
JOHN CLARK

■

THE CONSERVATION FOUNDATION
Washington, D. C.

In cooperation with

National Oceanic and Atmospheric Administration
Office of Coastal Environment
U.S. Department of Commerce

The Conservation Foundation is a nonprofit organization dedicated to encouraging human conduct to sustain and enrich life on earth. Since its founding in 1948, it has attempted to provide intellectual leadership in the cause of wise management of the earth's resources. It is now focusing increasing attention on one of the critical issues of the day— how to use wisely that most basic resource, the land itself.

*   *   *

John Clark, the author of this book, was Senior Associate of The Conservation Foundation. He is a marine ecologist and ichthyologist. He was formerly with the Woods Hole Fishery Laboratory in Massachusetts and the Sandy Hook Marine Laboratory in New Jersey.

*   *   *

Library of Congress Card Catalogue Number 74-77717

ISBN: 0-89164-017-7

© *The Conservation Foundation, 1974*

Fourth Printing: September 1989

Book orders should be directed to The Conservation Foundation, P.O. Box 4866, Hampden Post Office, Baltimore, Maryland 21211. Telephone: (301) 338-6951.

ACKNOWLEDGMENTS

The support for the study upon which this guidebook is based came from two sources: the Office of Coastal Environment of the National Oceanic and Atmospheric Administration of the United States Department of Commerce (Grant No. 04-3-158-68) and the American Conservation Association, New York, N.Y. I am specifically grateful to Robert W. Knecht of the Office of Coastal Environment and to George R. Lamb of the American Conservation Association for their personal encouragement in this undertaking and to Roland S. Woolson, Jr., of John Wiley and Sons, for approval to publish this shortened version of a comprehensive reference book on the subject which the company intends to publish. Dr. Edward T. LaRoe of the Office of Coastal Environment devoted considerable personal time and effort to the improvement of the manuscript, for which I am deeply appreciative.

Others who gave so generously of their time to reviewing and criticizing the manuscript were: Joseph MacDonald, Richard Gardner, Dr. Marc Hershman, Dr. D. Rodney Mack, Ms. E. Ellington, William Taylor, John Capper, Dr. Frank Bowerman, Charles Tucker, Joe C. Mosely II, Matthew B. Connolly, Rick Smarden, and Crane Miller, Esq.

Those at the Conservation Foundation whose personal efforts during the course of this work are deeply appreciated include: Mrs. Laura O'Sullivan, Paul Sarokwash, Carl Nelson and Trevor O'Neill.

TABLE OF CONTENTS

INTRODUCTION

The purpose of this guidebook is to reduce a vast stockpile of ecological data to a few simple principles, by means of which to improve our use of coastal lands and waters. The need for improvement should be apparent to anyone who has examined a number of the Nation's coastal ecosystems and found true a Federal report that all but 25 percent of them are seriously degraded by the polluting effects of civilization.

We take the view that environmental management of coastal waters and shorelands has as one of its fundamental goals the maintenance of coastal ecosystems at the highest achievable level of quality, which means as near the natural condition as possible or, as we state it, at the level of *best achievable ecosystem function.*

Starting with a foundation of fundamental Ecologic Principles we have developed for this guidebook a number of general Management Rules and suggested a variety of constraints on coastal development activities. These constraints are aimed at specific uses of coastal waters and shore-lands such as agriculture, marinas, residential development, and so forth.

It is not within the scope of this guidebook to present a great deal of background data nor an examination of the merits of different opinions or scientific results. However, a fuller presentation will be made in our subsequent, more comprehensive, book on this subject to be published by John Wiley and Sons, Interscience. In many respects the present guidebook is a preliminary effort in a new and undeveloped discipline.

Whatever its specific goals may be an environmental management program must embrace whole ecosystems. Any attempt to manage separately one of the many interdependent components of a complex ecosystem will very likely fail. So would any attempt to control any one source of disturbance to the system (such as upland erosion), without controlling others (such as dredging or marsh filling).

In the preparation of a management plan for any coastal area, it will be necessary to make a professional analysis of each coastal ecosystem to determine its values and vulnerabilities and to devise effective controls on potentially adverse activities. The framework for a management analysis of an ecosystem must include not only the important biota but the major physical factors and the effect of each on the functioning of the ecosystem, how these factors interact and how in combination they affect the life of the system.

The ecosystem defined for management purposes must embrace a complete and integral unit of interactive natural forces. This means a unit including not only a coastal water basin (or basins) but also the adjacent shorelands to the extent of their having significant influence on coastal waters. In short, the basic unit of coastal management is a single intact and complete ecosystem including the coastal water basin and the related adjacent shorelands.

It is necessary to include the adjacent shoreland watershed for a very practical purpose: the flow of water from the land is a primary controlling factor on the condition of coastal ecosystems. Therefore, maintenance of the quality and quantity of runoff through regulation of land use practice is critical.

Ecosystems of the confined estuarine water basins are usually ecologically complex and exceptionally rich: "Characteristically, estuaries tend to be more productive than either the sea on one side or the freshwater drainage on the other" (E. P. Odum).[1]

One also finds that estuaries are the most sensitive and stress-vulnerable coastal ecosystems of the confined water bodies—particularly those with poor circulation properties.

Development adjacent to estuarine waters will require exceptionally vigorous management attention. For this reason we have given a higher degree of attention to estuaries than to ocean water areas. However, we have also focused attention on those especially rich and vulnerable life systems of the ocean that require protection, such as coral reefs and kelp beds.

Although we have not specifically addressed the Great Lakes, many of the principles applying to marine estuaries will be found to apply to the ecosystems of the Great Lakes.

While scientists can state what conditions are optimum for best ecosystem function, they are not equipped to offer advice on what constitutes socially acceptable or unacceptable levels of degradation of ecosystems. Moreover, they have rarely had the opportunity to collect enough data to predict, quantitatively, the response of an ecosystem to a specific disturbance. In effect, ecological scientists can establish the criteria upon which to judge ecosystem condition and upon which public decision-making shall proceed, but are not themselves qualified to make the decisions.

In this spirit we attempt to provide a comprehensive ecological background for decision-making and to suggest a framework for management practice which will lead to the *best achievable ecosystem function*. How far short of this goal any management program falls must of necessity be decided by society not by science.

SUMMARY

Environmental management of coastal waters and shorelands has as one of its fundamental goals the maintenance of coastal ecosystems in their best condition, or at the level of *best achievable ecosystem function,* which usually means as near to the natural condition as possible.

Whatever its specific goals may be an environmental management program must embrace whole ecosystems. Any attempt to manage separately one of the many interdependent components of a complex ecosystem will very likely fail. So would any attempt to control any one source of environmental disturbance to the system without controlling others. The ecosystem defined must embrace a complete and integral unit, one that includes a coastal water basin (or basins) and the adjacent shorelands to the extent they have significant influence on coastal waters.

Development adjacent to estuarine waters will require exceptionally vigorous management attention. For this reason we have given a higher degree of attention to estuaries than to ocean water areas. Many of the principles applying to marine estuaries will be found to apply to the ecosystems of the Great Lakes, not specifically addressed here.

This summary comprises the findings and recommendations derived from the main text of the guidebook. The page number citations serve as an index and locator to particular topics of interest.

AREA DESIGNATION

Planning requires a system of identification and classification of general *areas of environmental concern* (page 88). These are areas within which human activities must be controlled, *not necessarily prohibited,* to protect the environment. Smaller areas that are especially critical ecologically—*vital areas*—are to be designated for complete protection *within* areas of concern (page 59). Estuaries and their surrounding tidelands and wetlands are *areas of environmental concern* (page 90). Coastal flood plains also are designated as *areas of environmental concern* because of their relation to coastal waters (page 95). Shorelands above the flood plain may be thought of as *areas of normal concern* (page 93).

A designation system closely parallel to ours has the following three categories: (1) preservation (or protection), (2) conservation, and (3) utilization (or development) (page 91).

A brief explanation of each comparable set of capability designations and its implications follows:

1. *Vital Areas* or Preservation Areas: Ecosystem elements of such critical importance and high value that they are to be preserved intact and protected from harmful outside forces—encompassed *within* an *area of environmental concern.*

2. *Areas of Environmental Concern* or Conservation Areas: Broad areas of environmental sensitivity, often containing one or more *vital areas,* the development or use of which must be carefully controlled to protect the ecosystem.

3. *Areas of Normal Concern* or Utilization Areas: Areas where only the normal levels of caution are required in utilization and in development activity.

ECOLOGIC PRINCIPLES

Eleven principles derived from ecology that underlie major management functions are given below:

1. *Ecosystem integrity*—No one part of an ecosystem operates independently of any other (page 1).

2. *Linkage*—Water provides the essential linkage of land and sea elements of the coastal ecosystem (page 4).

3. *Inflow*—The natural volume, pattern, and seasonal rate of fresh water inflow provides for optimum ecosystem function (page 10).

4. *Basin circulation*—The natural pattern of water circulation within basins provides for optimum ecosystem function (page 16).

5. *Energy*—The flow and amount of available energy governs life processes within the coastal ecosystem (page 31).

6. *Storage*—A high capability for energy storage provides for optimum ecosystem function (page 33).

7. *Nitrogen*—Productivity in coastal waters is normally governed by the amount of available nitrogen (page 19).

8. *Light*—The natural light regime provides for optimum ecosystem function (page 22).

9. *Temperatures*—The natural temperature regime provides for optimum ecosystem function (page 22).

10. *Oxygen*—High concentrations of dissolved oxygen provide for optimum ecosystem function (page 19).

11. *Salinity*—The natural salinity regime provides for optimum ecosystem function (page 17).

MANAGEMENT PRINCIPLES AND RULES

The following fifteen Management Rules and Principles are founded upon the Ecologic Principles and are the basis for the practical series of Recommended Constraints on specific uses given in Chapter 4 of the main text:

Management Principles

1. *Ecosystem integrity:* Each coastal ecosystem must be managed with respect to the relatedness of its parts and the unity of its whole (page 25).

2. *Drainage:* A fundamental goal of shoreland management is to retain the system of land drainage as near to the natural pattern as possible (page 42).

3. *Drainageway buffers:* The need to provide vegetative buffer area along drainageways increases with the degree of development (page 40).

4. *Wetlands and tidelands:* The need to preserve wetlands and vegetated tidelands increases with the degree of development (page 73).

5. *Storage:* Storage components of ecosystems are of extreme value and should always be fully protected (page 33).

6. *Energy:* To maintain an ecosystem at optimum function it is necessary to protect and optimize the sources and flows of energy that power the system (page 32).

Management Rules

1. *Drainageways:* Alteration of any drainageway by realignment, bulkheading, filling, impounding, or any other process that shortcuts the natural rate or pattern

of flow or blocks or impedes its passage is unacceptable (page 40).

2. *Basin circulation:* Any significant change from the natural rate of water flows of a coastal water basin is presumed to be ecologically detrimental and is unacceptable (page 42).

3. *Nutrient supply:* Reduction of the natural supply of nutrients to the coastal ecosystem by alteration of fresh water inflow is unacceptable (page 38).

4. *Nitrogen:* Discharge of nitrogenous compounds into confined coastal waters is presumed to have adverse effects through eutrophication and is unacceptable (page 19).

5. *Turbidity:* Turbidity of higher than natural levels is to be presumed detrimental to the coastal ecosystem and is unacceptable (page 22).

6. *Temperature:* Significant alteration of the natural temperature regime of the coastal ecosystem is presumed adverse and is unacceptable (page 22).

7. *Oxygen:* Any significant reduction from the natural concentration of oxygen is presumed to be adverse and is unacceptable (page 20).

8. *Salinity:* Any significant change from the natural salinity regime is presumed ecologically detrimental and is unacceptable (page 39).

9. *Runoff contamination:* Any significant discharge of suspended solids, nutrients, or toxic chemicals is to be presumed adverse and is unacceptable (page 38).

Controls

Because both land and water use controls are necessary for *best achievable ecosystem function,* it is necessary to regulate both the location and the design of projects in shoreland and coastal water provinces. Also, many types of human activities must be controlled to some degree. In addition, the construction of many types of projects and their operations will have to conform to certain performance standards. The basis for the necessary controls is detailed in the main text along with 88 Recommended Constraints on specific uses.

Program Elements

Environmental management for the coastal zone should be organized around maintenance at optimum levels of the known properties of the ecosystem, including its features, characteristics, and processes. Planning and management activities should include the following eleven Program Elements:

1. *Vital areas:* Ecologically critical areas with high value value for storage, primary productivity, habitat and water purification or regulation.

2. *Fresh water inflow:* The volume, quality, and rate of delivery to coastal waters of water from outside the coastal management district.

3. *Watershed drainage:* The factors governing the volume, quality, and rate of delivery of fresh water to coastal waters from the coastal watershed.

4. *Circulation:* Maintenance of the natural patterns of water movement throughout the coastal water basin.

5. *Nutrients:* Control of the sources and disposition of naturally occurring and introduced nutrients.

6. *Sediments:* Control of the sources of sediments from the shorelands, coastal basins and inland areas.

7. *Clarity:* Control of water turbidity.

8. *Temperature:* Control of sources of anomalous heating of coastal waters.

9. *Oxygen:* Maintenance of high levels of dissolved oxygen in coastal waters.

10. *Salinity:* Maintenance of the natural patterns of salinity in coastal waters.

11. *Toxics:* Control of sources of toxic discharges to coastal waters.

CHAPTER 1

Ecologic Considerations

Ecology is the science which relates living forms to their environment. In this sense, the environment of a species includes not only physical forces, but all the other species present. As it is used here, ecology has the broad connotation of treating whole communities of life. Our discussion focuses on the ecosystem—the basic functional geographic unit that embraces all of the life and physical components of one distinct interacting unit of shoreland and adjacent coastal waters. Ecosystem orientation stresses that management of coastal water areas, to be effective, must be coupled with management of adjacent shorelands and fresh water sources. This approach is built on the following Ecological Principle: *No one part of an ecosystem operates independently of any other.*

ESTUARINE SYSTEMS

The term *estuary* has a variety of definitions but as we use it here: *An estuary is any confined coastal water body with an open connection to the sea and a measurable quantity of salt in its waters.* We use this definition of estuary in preference to one which includes only those enclosed water bodies that receive a *significant* fresh water input. This simpler definition includes all enclosed coastal waters and avoids the problem of setting lagoons aside from estuaries because of a particular rate of inflow from the land. Where it is necessary to make the distinction, lagoons can be separately considered as one of many types of estuary. Consequently, our definition agrees with that of E. P. Odum[1] (as modified from D. W. Pritchard[2]): ". . . a semi-enclosed coastal body of water which has a free connection to the sea; it is thus strongly affected by tidal action, and within it sea water is mixed (and usually measurably diluted) with fresh water from land drainage."

When we use the term "confined" to describe one property of the estuary we recognize that at some point even the most landlocked estuary has an opening and thus might be technically termed partially confined or semi-enclosed. Where, for management purposes, one might wish to use a rule of thumb to distinguish between estuarine and open ocean

1

areas based upon the degree of confinement, we suggest the following: *A confined coastal waterbody, or estuary, is one that has a shoreline length in excess of three times the width of its outlet to the sea.*

The exceptional natural value of the estuarine type of ecosystem derives from a beneficial combination of physical properties that separately or in combination perform such functions as those listed below:

1. *Confinement:* Provides shelter which protects the estuary from wave action and allows plants to root, clams to set and permits retention of suspended life and nutrients.
2. *Depth:* Allows light to penetrate to plants on the bottom; fosters growth of marsh plants and tideflat biota; discourages oceanic predators which avoid shallow waters.
3. *Salinity:* Fresh water flow may create a distinct surface layer over a saltier, heavier, bottom layer, thus inducing beneficial stratified flow; fresh water dilution deters oceanic predators and encourages estuarine forms.
4. *Circulation:* Sets up a beneficial system of transport for suspended life, when stratified, such that the bottom layer flows in and the surface layer flows out; enhances flushing; retains organisms in favorable habitats through behavior adaptations.
5. *Tide:* Tidal energy provides an important driving force; tidal flow transports nutrients and suspended life, dilutes and flushes wastes; tidal rhythm acts as an important regulator of feeding, breeding, and other functions.
6. *Nutrient storage:* Trapping mechanisms store nutrients within the estuary; marsh and grass beds store nutrients for slow release as detritus; richness induces high accumulation of available nutrients in animal tissue.

THE PHYSICAL SETTING

Each coastal ecosystem operates within the confines of a particular basin (or basins) formed by the geologic structure of the coast—a straight shoreline, a deep rocky fiord, a tidal river, or a shallow marshy embayment. Similarly, the shoreland section of the ecosystem operates within the topographic confines of the watershed. The characteristics of the emergent and submergent counterparts—shorelands and basin bottom—are geologically related, as fixed by the general shape, size and depth of

coastal water bodies. The enduring geologic characteristics are themselves modified somewhat by the dynamic forces of water flow, waves
and wind, erosion and sedimentation, and by the effects of vegetation.

A wide continental shelf is generally associated with extensive low-
lying shorelands and a wide band of wetlands next to the coast, while a
narrow shelf is associated with steep or mountainous shorelands. These
associations and their characteristic estuarine systems differ greatly from
one coastal region to another.

Northern shores once covered by ice—New England, Puget Sound, and
southeast Alaska—are sharply sculptured with generally steep shorelines
and have deep, heavily indented embayments, islands, steep rocky shores
and irregular bottom topography.[3] These characteristics generally extend
to unglaciated parts of the Pacific Coast.

The parts of the Atlantic and Gulf coasts that were unaffected by
glaciation consist of relatively flat terrain in which wide coastal embayments and marshes are the predominant features. These are coasts formed
primarily of sediments eroded from ancient mountains, and along which
embayments and marshes form traps for sediments the rivers bring down
to the sea. Characterized by great expanses of shallow water and aquatic
vegetation, these coasts have extensive sand dunes, sandy ocean beachfront, and well developed estuaries behind them.

The constant input of sediments from erosion tends to fill up the estuary
basin. In time, deltas may be formed, stretching out into the sea. The
highest concentrations of sediment carried by estuarine waters are found
in the inner, low-salinity, portion. Here, salt water meets fresh, coalescing
river-borne silts into larger, heavier, particles which settle out as the
estuary broadens and the flow slackens (Figure 1).

The geologic form of the water basin controls the coastal ecosystem
largely through secondary effects; that is, by influencing such factors as
currents, temperature, vegetation, and *flushing rate* (the rate of replacement of water in the basin). For example, the structure of a typical
estuary sets up a pattern of currents which retains nutrients—a condition
favorable to the development of a rich and varied community of life.

The effect on a coastal water ecosystem of any particular environmental
stress depends partly, sometimes largely, on the geologic form of the
ecosystem basin and the ecologic characteristics induced by that form.
Furthermore, subsystems of each ecosystem may be expected to react
differently to any particular disturbance (Figure 2).

The coastal waters of the United States may be conveniently divided
into large biogeographical regions. These regions vary in such factors as:
climatic condition, the oceanographic characteristics of the seas that

3

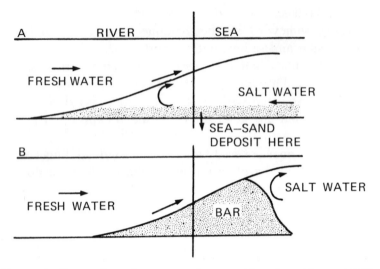

Figure 1. Formation of an estuarine sand bar (van Veen, 1950).[4]

border them, and in the way they are influenced by the type of land mass that lies behind them. Of climatic variables, temperature is the primary determinant of the distribution of species of plants and animals throughout the coastal zone. Other significant climatic factors are the amount and pattern of precipitation, of wind, and of sunlight. Large-scale oceanic forces that influence coastal ecosystems are prevailing wind and waves, permanent coastal currents, persistent coastal upwellings, massive oceanic warm water currents, and other factors that vary from place to place along the coast. Most climatic and oceanic forces are beyond significant human control. But man can significantly control the ways in which land influences coastal ecosystems.

SHORELANDS

The primary ecological consideration in coastal management is control of water. This applies not only to coastal waters but to the upland *drainageways* and to the land surfaces. It implies that the natural patterns of land vegetation and drainage are to be retained in land development. It is necessary to respect this basic Ecological Principle: *Water provides the essential linkage of land and sea elements of the coastal ecosystem.*

The basic hydrologic forces at work in the shorelands (Figure 3) are familiar to hydrologists, civil engineers, and planners, and understanding them requires little special knowledge. However, understanding the basic

4

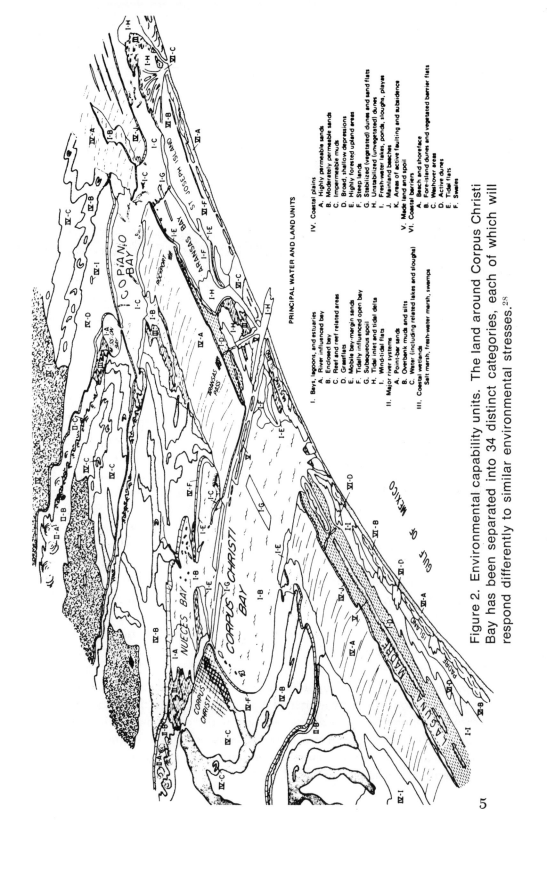

PRINCIPAL WATER AND LAND UNITS

I. Bays, lagoons, and estuaries
   A. River influenced bay
   B. Enclosed bay
   C. Reef and reef related areas
   D. Grassflats
   E. Mobile bay-margin sands
   F. Tidally influenced open bay
   G. Subaqueous spoil
   H. Tidal inlet and tidal delta
   I. Wind-tidal flats

II. Major river systems
   A. Point-bar sands
   B. Overbank muds and silts
   C. Water (including fresh-water lakes and sloughs)

III. Coastal wetlands
   Salt marsh, fresh-water marsh, swamps

IV. Coastal plains
   A. Highly permeable sands
   B. Moderately permeable sands
   C. Impermeable muds
   D. Broad, shallow depressions
   E. Highly forested upland areas
   F. Steep lands
   G. Stabilized (vegetated) dunes and sand flats
   H. Unstabilized (unvegetated) dunes
   I. Fresh-water lakes, ponds, sloughs, playas
   J. Mainland beaches
   K. Areas of active faulting and subsidence

V. Made land and spoil

VI. Coastal barriers
   A. Beach and shoreface
   B. Fore-island dunes and vegetated barrier flats
   C. Washover areas
   D. Active dunes
   E. Tidal flats
   F. Swales

Figure 2. Environmental capability units. The land around Corpus Christi Bay has been separated into 34 distinct categories, each of which will respond differently to similar environmental stresses.[28]

5

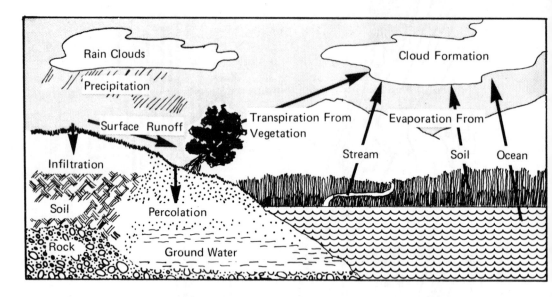

Figure 3. The hydrologic cycle.[6]

forces at work in coastal waters—tides, density layers, reversing currents —and how they react with the ecosystem, does require special knowledge. Therefore, the assistance of particular expertise in the area of hydrography, or oceanography, will usually be required in coastal zone planning.

Coastal waters are a mixture of fresh water from the land and salt water from the sea. The workings of the coastal ecosystem are influenced by characteristics of both sources of water supply, by the forces that drive them, and by the interplay between them. In a way, the two sources are in competition for the space within the enclosed water basins.

The ocean source, with a giant reservoir of water and power behind it, pushes steadily inward against the lighter and usually more variable force of the land source. While the ocean flow is modified somewhat by tide levels, storms, and changes in inlet size, the river flow is considerably more variable because of seasonal changes in precipitation and runoff.

In the context of this competition then, the ocean water forces apply rather consistent pressure for estuarine space while the land water forces apply more fluctuating amounts of pressure. For this reason, one looks to the land source—the watershed—for an explanation of intermittent, or seasonal changes in such characteristics of the estuarine environment as salinity, circulation patterns and water content. There is another reason to be concerned with the land sources—they are the ones we constantly alter and can most easily control.

6

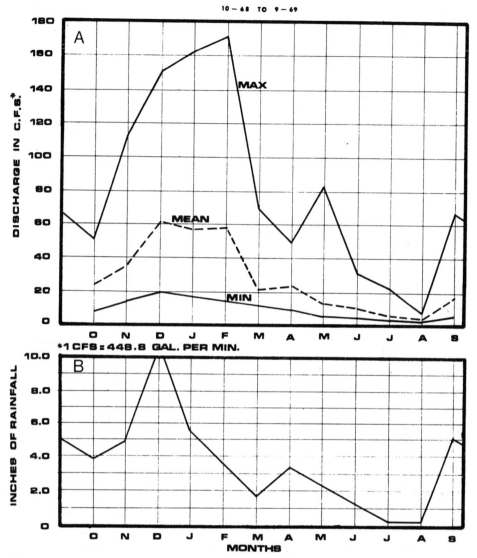

Figure 4. Mercer Creek, tributary to Lake Washington and Puget Sound (Oct. 1968 to Sept. 1969). A = stream discharge, B = monthly precipitation.[6]

All lands which are periodically covered by salty water because of tidal or normal storm action are part of the coastal waters complex. These are the *tidelands* and *wetlands;* they belong to the province of the sea and the estuary. Landward of this transition zone is the *coastal flood plain,* the shoreland area inundated only by hurricanes or infrequent large storms. Upland of the flood plain are the *shorelands* proper, all lands

7

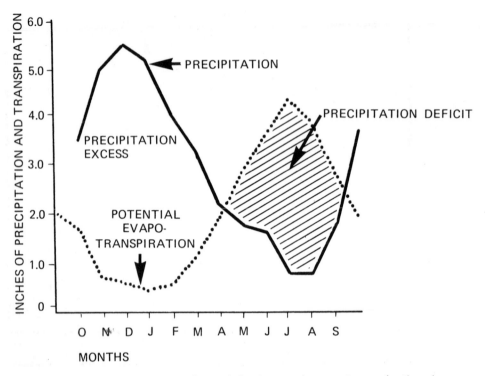

Figure 5. A typical pattern of precipitation and evapotranspiration (combined evaporation and transpiration).[6]

that drain *directly* into coastal waters. In addition to wetlands, tidelands, and water basins, any plan for coastal zone management must include the shorelands (with their coastal flood plains), because they strongly influence coastal waters through the water exchange process and are in turn strongly influenced by coastal waters. Therefore each defined coastal ecosystem must include all shorelands of its drainage system—the complete watershed—in order to be complete and functional for management purposes.

Water moves seaward over the land by one of three types of flow: channeled flow, surface (sheet) flow, or sub-surface (underground) flow. Management considerations may be different for each mode of flow. The easiest type to manage is channeled flow; but specific guidelines can be developed for the two other modes as well.

The amount of fresh water arriving in a particular coastal ecosystem varies seasonally (Figure 4). The size of the flow is a function of the size of the watershed and interplay between rainfall and the rates of loss to the atmosphere via *evapotranspiration* (water transpired by trees, shrubs

8

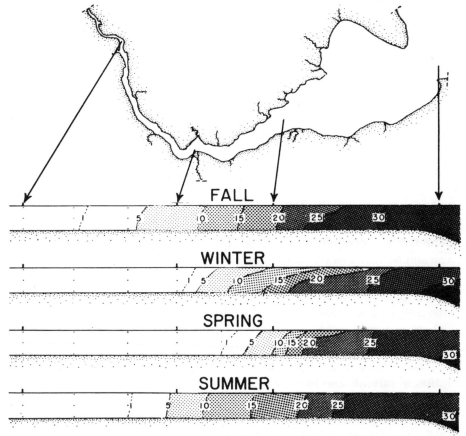

Figure 6. Salinity in the Delaware Estuary.[7] Numbers refer to the salinity as amount of salts in parts per thousand of water (ppt).

and plants, and evaporation), both of which vary seasonally in a more or less predictable manner (Figure 5). The annual variations in these factors cause ecologically important year-to-year differences in the flow to coastal waters.

The volume of the fresh water supply governs the salinity of all coastal waters. Salinity influences the types of species and their abundance and therefore the whole distribution of life throughout coastal waters—fish, shellfish, plankton, plants, and bottom fauna. Normally the salinity gradient established in an estuary fluctuates with the amount of river discharge. The location of any specific salinity in the tidal river portion of a large estuary may vary by 10 to 20 miles or more depending on the amount of fresh water discharge from upstream (Figure 6).

The volume of fresh water inflow also governs the pattern of circulation of coastal waters through the rate of flushing of water basins and the

9

strength of currents. In a stratified (two-layered) estuary the amount of runoff controls both the surface layer outflow and the bottom layer inflow. Circulation strongly influences the abundance and the pattern of distribution of life in the estuary.

Also related to volume is the amount of sediment, nutrient, minerals, organic matter, and other substances dissolved or suspended in the water and carried down into the estuary. These materials have a strong influence on the quality of the coastal ecosystem because they affect plant production, oxygen concentration, and the fallout of sediments in estuarine basins. Figure 7 shows how nutrients (ammonia, nitrate, and nitrite) and oxygen are related in the fresh water and brackish parts of a tidal river. Nutrients supplied naturally via runoff are an important part of the energy budget of many coastal ecosystems.

The rate or schedule of the flow of fresh water into coastal waters is governed by many of the same factors that govern the volume of the flow. The schedule of flow is important in its effect on the productivity, stability, and general health of the coastal ecosystem. The natural rhythm or pattern of seasonal flow is generally beneficial.

There are predictable seasonal variations in river flow into the coastal waters of the United States. The total volumes of inflow reflect not only the total amount of precipitation, and evapotranspiration, but the interception of rainfall and the sizes and slopes of the watershed (Figure 8). The detention characteristics of the terrain over which the runoff waters flow enroute to the river channel are also important in governing the rate of delivery; for example, it may take from three to four months for rainwater that falls in the south central Florida area to move 60-80 miles south to the estuarine areas around Florida Bay. While rain moves directly into the hydrologic system as ground water or surface runoff, snow and ice may remain for months, subsequently causing an influx of many months' precipitation when it melts.

The above considerations lead to the following Ecologic Principle: *The natural volume, pattern and seasonal rate of fresh water inflow provides for optimum ecosystem function.* Therefore, it should become standard management practice to maintain intact the natural pattern of fresh water inflow.

THE COASTAL WATERS

The ecologic health of each coastal ecosystem is controlled by oceanic and terrestrial factors that influence the condition of its waters. A primary factor, and one that gives each ecosystem its particular character, is the pattern of fresh water inflow. Other important factors which

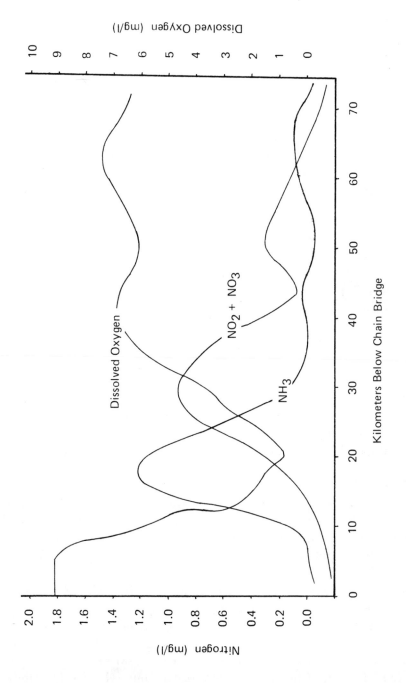

Figure 7. Ammonia (NH₃) and nitrate-nitrite concentrations (Aug. 19-22, 1968) and dissolved oxygen concentration (Sept. 22, 1968). (The Chain Bridge is 5 miles upriver from downtown Washington, D. C.).[8]

11

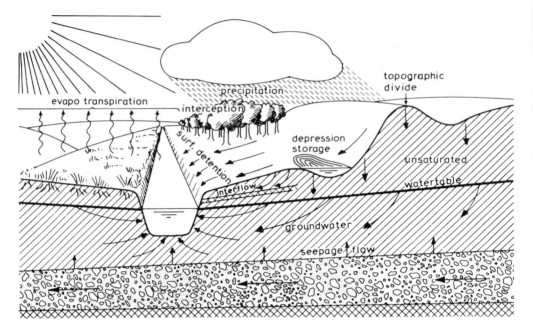

Figure 8. The riverine hydrologic cycle.[5]

control the dynamic physical processes of coastal ecosystems are tidal forces and currents. Inner needs of the system are supplied by constituents of the water—dissolved chemicals, suspended solids, and dissolved gasses.

Water Circulation

The combined influences of fresh water flow, tidal action, wind, and oceanic forces result in the specific pattern of water movement, or circulation, found in any coastal ecosystem. Circulation of water transports nutrients, propels plankton, spreads "seed" stages (planktonic larvae of fish and shellfish), flushes the wastes from animal and plant life, cleanses the system of pollutants, controls salinity, shifts sediments about, mixes the water and performs other useful work.

Circulation patterns in offshore ocean waters are dominated by large-scale forces which may have far distant origins, such as massive currents like the Gulf Stream or California Current. More localized influences may be important in the nearshore ocean zone where tide, wind, waves and land runoff are forces that control longshore currents, coastal upwelling of bottom waters, prevailing longshore currents, and various reverse flows, eddies, and tiderips.

12

Biophysical region	Type of tide	Tidal range (feet) Mean	Spring	Diurnal [1]	Maximum tidal flood	Current velocity ebb
North Atlantic:						
Eastport, Maine (Bay of Fundy)	Equal semidiurnal	18.2	20.7		3.5	3.5
Isle de Haut, Maine: (Penobscot Bay)	do	9.3	10.7		1.6	1.7
Portsmouth Harbor, N.H.	do	8.7	10.0		1.4	2.1
Boston Harbor, Mass.	do	9.5	11.0		2.0	1.5
Middle Atlantic:						
Dumpling Rocks (Buzzard Bay)	do	3.7	4.6		.9	1.3
The Narrows (New York Harbor)	do	4.5	5.5		2.0	2.3
Cape May Harbor, N.J.	do	4.4	5.3		2.1	2.5
Virginia Beach, Va.	do	3.4	.1		1.3	.9.
Chesapeake Bay:						
Wolf Trap Light (lower bay)	do	1.0	1.2		1.8	2.2
Point No Point (midbay)	do	1.3	1.5		.5	.7
Chesapeake Bay Bridge, Maryland	do	.8	.9		.8	1.0
Washington, D.C. (Potomac River)	do	2.9	3.3		.7	.3
South Atlantic:						
Wilmington, N.C. (Cape Fear River)	do	3.6	3.9		2.0	1.7
Savannah River entrance, Georgia	do	6.9	8.1		1.8	3.0
Mayport, Fla. (St. Johns River)	do	4.5	5.3		2.5	3.5
Fort Pierce Inlet, Fla.	do	2.6	3.0		3.0	3.5
Caribbean:						
Miami Harbor, Fla.	do	2.5	3.0		2.2	2.4
Key West, Fla.	do	1.3	1.6		1.2	2.0
San Juan, P.R.	do	1.1	1.3		(2)	(2)
Christiansted, St. Croix	Diurnal			0.8	(2)	(2)
Gulf of Mexico:						
St. Petersburg, Fla. (Tampa Bay)	do			2.3	.3	.3
Pensacola Bay entrance, Florida	do			1.1	1.8	2.1
Barataria Bay, La.	do			.9	1.7	1.7
Aransas Pass, Tex.	do			1.7	1.6	1.0
Pacific Southwest:						
Sen Diego Bay entrance, California	Unequal semidiurnal	3.9		5.6	1.2	1.4
Monterey Bay, Calif.	do	3.5		5.3	(2)	(2)
San Francisco Bay entrance, California.	do	4.0		5.7	3.3	3.9
Point Arena, Calif.	do	4.0		5.8	1.3	1.3
Pacific Northwest:						
Humboldt Bay entrance, California	do	4.5		6.4	1.8	2.3
Yaquina Bay entrance, Oregon	do	5.9		7.9	2.8	2.6
Grays Harbor entrance, Washington	do	6.9		9.0	2.5	2.2
Puget Sound (Elliott Bay), Wash.	do	7.6		11.3	(2)	(2)
Alaska:						
Juneau (Gastineau Channel)	do	13.8		16.4	2.3	2.3
Anchorage (Cook Inlet)	do	25.1		28.1	3.3	3.3
Goodnews Bay (Kuskokwim Bay)	do	6.2		8.9	2.6	2.4
Point Barrow	do	.3		.4	(2)	(2)
Pacific Islands:						
Honolulu, Hawaii (Oahu)	do	1.2		1.9	(3)	(3)
Hilo, Hawaii (Hawaii)	do	1.6		2.4	(3)	(3)
Apra Harbor, Guam	do	(3)		(3)	1.7	3.4
Pago Pago Harbor, American Samoa	do	2.5		4.0	(3)	(3)

[1] For an unequal semidiurnal tide, the diurnal range is the extreme range over the 2 sequential tides in slightly over 1 day.
[2] Weak and variable.
[3] No data.

Reference: The National Estuarine Inventory.
Data source: U.S. Coast and Geodetic Survey.

Table 1. Typical tidal characteristics of the coastal zone of the United States.[3]

Tide is often the dominant force in water movement. Its amplitude, and therefore its strength in driving estuarine circulation, varies greatly with latitude and with certain ocean forces, as illustrated in Table 1. Amplitude varies within each system, decreasing inward from the ocean through the inlet to the head of the estuarine basin. It also varies with the shape, size, and even the bottom material of individual basins. Circulation forces tend to be greater and flushing rates better where tidal amplitudes are high.

13

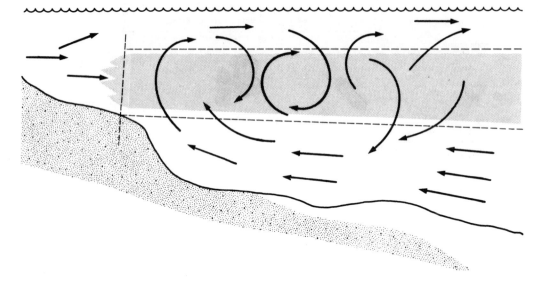

Figure 9. Circulation pattern in a typical stratified estuary.

In estuarine *lagoons* (shallow basins with little fresh water inflow and restricted openings), wind is often the only force effectively driving circulation, both in the process of mixing and of inducing currents. Lagoons are often poorly flushed and quite vulnerable to a buildup of contaminants and to other disturbances.

Stratified Estuaries

The *stratified* system of circulation is typical of many important estuaries and is the result of the intrusion of heavier salt water from the ocean (the "salt wedge") under the less saline and lighter outflow of water from the rivers. In this situation, common to deeper estuaries with high outward flow of fresh water, the bottom water is carried in toward the upper estuary (Figure 9). This creates in stratified estuaries the distinctive pattern of opposite flows that results in outward transport of surface organisms and inward transport of bottom organisms. These are "net" or "residual" flows—the net rate of movement after tidal influence is discounted. Many *plankton* species have developed mechanisms to utilize the opposite flows of the two layers for passive propulsion. (Plankton includes all the multitude of tiny organisms that remain suspended in the water, and swim weakly, if at all.) For example, a plankton organism may descend into the bottom layer to be propelled up the estuary or move a few yards upward into the surface layer to go toward the sea. In this manner of strategic vertical movement, the organism can maintain itself

14

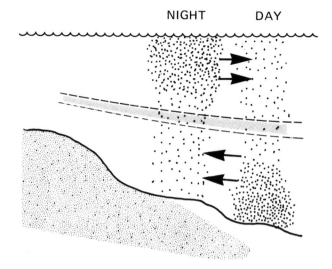

NIGHT   DAY

Figure 10. Strategic natural changes in the night and day distribution of estuarine zooplankton favors their concentration in mid-estuary.

in the most favorable part of the estuary. The result of the stratified circulation system, as we have observed it, is to allow plankton to concentrate most heavily in the middle and upper parts of the estuary. For this and other reasons, the middle and upper parts are the richest of the estuary and a place where life abounds.

This recycling of suspended forms makes them especially vulnerable to a variety of development impacts because they have repeated exposure. Many forms migrate up and down each day and night and they are alternatively carried up the estuary by the net bottom flow and then down by the net surface flow (Figure 10).

The two-layered flow system does not normally occur in lagoons, nor does it occur in shallow estuaries where the water is mixed by wind and tide from surface to bottom.

A flow counterpart does exist in the coastal ocean where temperature and salinity differences cause a layering of surface and bottom waters in depths greater than 25 or 30 feet. Near shore, the bottom layer often moves toward the coast while the surface layer moves away from the coast. Plankton move shoreward by descending into the bottom layer.

Good circulation connotes good environmental conditions. A high rate of flushing, usually considered beneficial, provides transport of nutrients, cleanses the natural system and performs other vital functions. Good flushing also protects ecosystems stressed by development, to some extent,

15

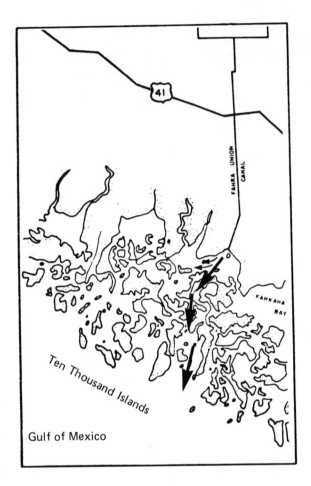

Figure 11. Fahka Union Bay and Canal, Collier County, Florida (main rate of freshwater discharge shown by arrows).[11]

because it hastens the dispersal and dilution of pollution. But, there is a limit beyond which the water passes too quickly through the system. For example, a large canal in southwest Florida forces water so rapidly through Fahka Union Bay that the mangrove system has a reduced opportunity to assimilate the nutrients in the water and to store them for use at times of slow discharge (Figure 11). Again it is a matter of balance and one must start with the presumption that the natural condition is best and should be maintained.

These considerations lead to a basic Ecologic Principle: *The natural pattern of water circulation within basins provides for optimum ecosystem function.*

16

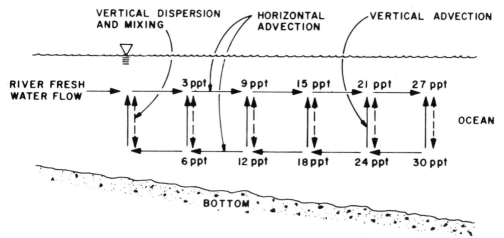

Figure 12. Salinity distribution and flow pathways in a typical stratified estuary.[12]

Salinity

The salinity of coastal waters reflects a complex mixture of dissolved salts, the most abundant of which is the common salt, sodium chloride. Ocean waters typically contain, in total, about 35 parts of salts per thousand parts of water (ppt). Salinity throughout the coastal ecosystem fluctuates with the amount of dilution by river inflow. Variations are most pronounced in the inner reaches of the estuary where the basin narrows into a tidal river. In most coastal areas, there is a gradient in salt content that starts with high values of 30 to 35 ppt along the outer coast and in the seaward ends of estuaries and drops to zero ppt at some distance up into the tributary tidal rivers. In stratified basins, deeper waters are saltier than surface waters (Figure 12).

Some coastal species tolerate a wide range of salinities, while others require a narrow range to live and reproduce successfully. Some species require different salinities at different phases of their life cycle such as are provided by regular seasonal rhythms in salinity caused by spring runoff, summer drought, etc. Figure 13 shows the range of salinity tolerance characteristic of some estuarine plants and animals. Most of those with a narrow tolerance can withstand short term exposure to a much wider salinity range, depending upon the rate of change. As with other environmental factors, coastal species have evolved over the years in harmony with their salinity environment and have adapted to the natural regime. The relevant Ecologic Principle is: *The natural salinity regime provides for optimum ecosystem function.*

17

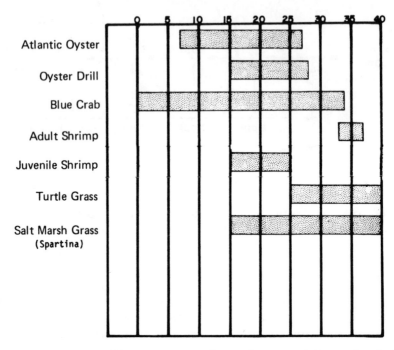

Figure 13. Salinity preference range for typical coastal species [adapted from ref. 3; data for juvenile shrimp (white and brown) added].

Other Chemical Constituents

The chemistry of coastal waters is complex because of the number of elements and compounds present and the multitude of ways in which they are involved with the biochemical processes of the diverse biota. The activities of mankind complicate the chemistry and result in the addition of nutrient salts, trace metals and other materials which either alter the natural system or poison the biota.

Important chemicals in coastal waters fall into two classes: nutrients and trace-elements. The nutrients are vital to the whole chain of life in coastal waters because they are required by all plants, whether rooted plants or microscopic *phytoplankton* (floating plant cells, algae), and because the animal life is supported by the plants (except for some direct nourishment of certain forms by dissolved organic nutrient). Free nutrient chemicals are relatively scarce in the waters of a natural coastal ecosystem because they are taken up rapidly by plant life (page 31). A supply of nutrient added to the system by natural processes (from

18

runoff, rainfall, or ocean sources), to replace losses keeps the system functioning optimally. This natural supply is a critical need and one cannot expect to successfully substitute for nature by providing an artificial supply.

The major plant nutrients are nitrate and phosphate with the nitrogen content of plant tissue being much higher than phosphorous.[13] In coastal waters (but not lakes), the amount of available nitrate is generally believed to be the nutrient factor that controls the abundance of plants.[14] The basic Ecologic Principle is: *Productivity in coastal waters is normally governed by the amount of available nitrogen.*

In normally productive coastal waters a significant increase in nitrogenous compounds from sewage or fertilizers, particularly nitrate, will lead to adverse eutrophication. This leads to the following Management Rule: *Discharge of nitrogenous compounds into confined coastal waters is presumed to have adverse effects through eutrophication and is unacceptable.*

Other dissolved substances of some importance are sulfate, carbonate, calcium, magnesium, sodium and potassium. Inorganic trace elements of importance in plant nutrition are iron, manganese, molybdenum, cobalt and zinc. Certain organic substances may also be critically involved, such as vitamins, organic compounds of nitrogen and simple sugars.

Dissolved Gasses in the Water

Of the various gasses that are found dissolved in coastal waters, those of greatest importance in the web of life are oxygen and carbon dioxide, both of which occur in small but vital quantities. Animals use oxygen and produce carbon dioxide. Plants use carbon dioxide and produce oxygen (on balance). Therefore, each form can benefit from the other's work—one's waste is the other's need. There is a critical balance in the cycle between plants and animals that also involves transfer of dissolved gasses across the water surface to and from the atmosphere (Figure 14).

For optimum ecosystem function, coastal waters need a *minimum* of 6 ppm of oxygen (six parts of dissolved oxygen per million of water, by weight).[15] The basic Ecologic Principle is: *High concentrations of dissolved oxygen provide for optimum ecosystem function.* There is little evidence to show that one need be concerned about harmful effects from *excess* oxygen in coastal systems.

The minimum oxygen required for healthy ecosystem function is maintained by natural processes in undisturbed coastal waters (except some confined estuaries during warm seasons). But oxygen may fall to unhealthy levels (less than 4 or 5 ppm), where sewage and other wastes

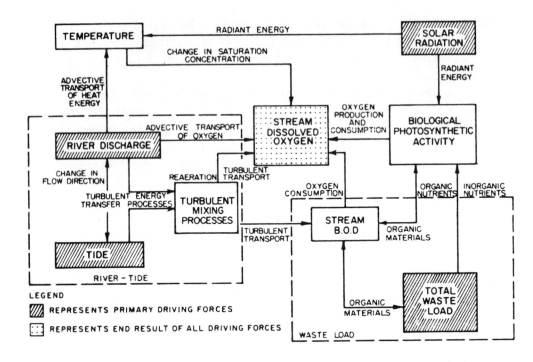

Figure 14. Factors affecting dissolved oxygen concentration in coastal waters.[3]

with high *biochemical oxygen demand* (BOD) pollute coastal waters and induce high bacterial action. The bacteria involved are common residents of coastal waters and are species which multiply rapidly to reach enormous abundance, thereby depleting the water of oxygen faster than it can be replaced by either plants or the atmosphere.

It is most necessary to include dissolved oxygen controls in the coastal management program. A specific goal should be to maintain an optimum oxygen environment, one that will normally be greater than the Federal minimum standard of 6 ppm (page 54). A basic Management Rule is: *Any significant reduction from the natural concentration of oxygen is presumed to be adverse and is unacceptable.*

The Function of Light

Sunlight is the basic driving force of the whole ecosystem. It is the fundamental source of energy for the growth of plants which in turn supply the foundation of nourishment for all life in coastal waters. For the ecosystem to function well, sunlight must be able to penetrate the

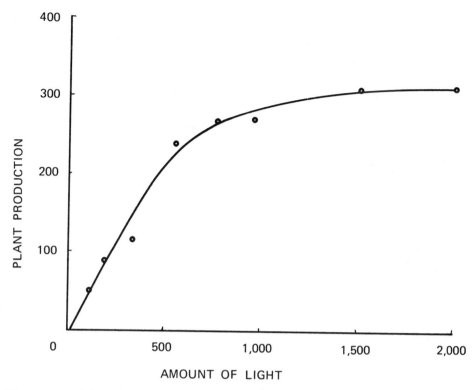

Figure 15. Relationships between plant production (gross primary production in mg. $O_2/m^2/hr.$) and light intensity (in ft. candles). Carbon dioxide concentration, 6.6 mg/l. (After McIntire and Phinney, 1965).[16]

water to a considerable depth so as to foster the growth of the rooted plants and the phytoplankton that float beneath the surface (Figure 15).

Turbidity from suspended silt or from concentrations of organisms has a negative effect on the amount of plant growth that can occur in coastal waters. In this way the growth of phytoplankton is self limiting; i.e., as it becomes denser the water becomes more turbid, decreasing the penetration of light into the water. Where light penetration is blocked by silt or by phytoplankton, there may be little plant growth occurring beneath a shallow surface layer. Estuaries are normally more turbid than ocean waters, being more silt laden and richer in nutrients and phytoplankton.

Light also affects the behavior of many animals. For example, many predatory gamefish are visual feeders and are benefitted by good light penetration. Conversely, the tiny young stages of many coastal fish seek refuge in estuarine waters to escape predators and turbidity may screen

21

them from attack. Neither extremely clear nor extremely murky water is the answer. Again, the solution is to maintain the natural condition, the environment in which the ecosystem has evolved and naturally prospered. Therefore, it is necessary to prevent the addition of silt that would block light penetration, or of nutrients that would stimulate excessive plankton growth and lead to this same condition. The appropriate Ecologic Principle is: *The natural light regime provides for optimum ecosystem function.*

Turbidity varies greatly with the seasons and with irregular environmental changes (freshets, winds, plankton blooms). Consequently, there will be no one base turbidity value but rather a complex pattern of variation which characterizes an ecosystem. The pattern will be difficult to pin down without extensive research. Therefore, an appropriate management plan is to reduce the *source* of turbidity to the minimum.

These considerations lead to the following Management Rule: *Turbidity of higher than natural level is to be presumed detrimental to the coastal ecosystem and is unacceptable.*

Water Temperature

Temperature exerts a major influence on the coastal ecosystem. The occurrence of any one species and the mix of whole coastal water communities of life tend to vary from north to south with changing temperature. Many functions of aquatic animals are temperature controlled; for example, migration, spawning, feeding efficiency, swimming speed, embryological development and basic metabolic rates (which double with each increase of 10°C (18°F).[17]

Temperature alteration—such as may be caused by power plant effluents or changes in waterflow patterns—is particularly critical in estuaries because life is so concentrated, and because so many important species resort to estuaries for certain key life functions.[18] The optimal temperature for any water habitat depends not only on the preferences of individual species but also on the well-being of the system as a whole. An ecological system is in dynamic balance and, like a finely tuned automobile engine, any damage to a single component can disable or impair the efficiency of the entire system.

The relevant Ecologic Principle is: *The natural temperature regime provides for optimum ecosystem function.* The appropriate Management Rule is: *Significant alteration of the natural temperature regime of the coastal ecosystem is presumed adverse and is unacceptable.*

BIOTA

The biota of coastal ecosystems includes a wide variety of plants, birds, fish, mammals and invertebrate organisms. Life is not only important for what it yields directly to mankind, but for the way it serves to keep the whole coastal water system in order. In its natural condition, the ecosystem incorporates a balanced network of biotic inter-relationships. The natural balance is all too easily upset by impacts from pollution and other major disturbances, which range from extreme damage to coastal life to serious degradation of the beauty and general utility of coastal waters.

Biotic Systems

The life system of the estuary begins with plant life—marsh grass, mangroves, submerged bottom plants or masses of drifting phytoplankton (frequently present in concentrations of millions per quart of water). Some of the plant material is consumed directly by shellfish and fish but more often it is first eaten by the *zooplankton* (tiny floating animal life) which in turn become the food of fishes, and they in turn are consumed by birds or people. This transfer of food energy from lower to higher forms, known as the *food chain* or *food web,* is comprised of a number of separate components. The plants are the *producers.* Smaller plant-eating animals, known as *consumers* (or herbivores), feed on the phyto-plankton or, to a lesser extent, on the larger plants. Others are *foragers,* those that prey directly on the consumers, and others are *predators,* those that prey on the foragers. A few species, including the finest game fish, are super-predators that pursue and capture smaller predators (Figure 16). Finally, there are the *decomposers,* bacteria that reduce dead matter back into basic minerals.

Many species change their feeding habits dramatically, utilizing different parts of the food chain as they grow from larvae to post-larvae to juveniles to adult fish. A sea trout might depend successively on crustacean larvae, copepods, small shrimps, bait fish, and eventually larger fish, crabs and other invertebrates.

Rooted plants are vital in the food system of estuaries (page 68). For example, in the tideland marshes or mangrove forests, as the grasses die or the mangrove leaves fall, the decaying plants create organic *detritus,* small organic particles which are spread by waterflow throughout the ecosystem to become an important nutrient element in the diet of many species. Beds of submerged grasses—eel grass, etc.,—also produce the valuable detritus.

23

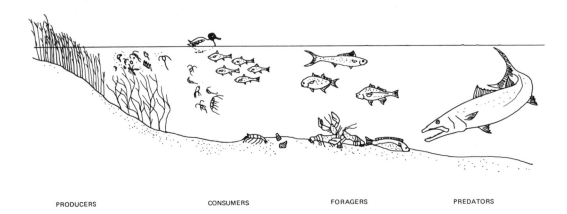

| PRODUCERS | CONSUMERS | FORAGERS | PREDATORS |

Figure 16. The food chain, or food web, in its basic form depicts the ecological system that provides food for fish, shellfish, and ultimately for man.[19] (Nan Nelson)

Much of the protein food of smaller aquatic animals is derived from digesting the bacteria and other microorganisms that live on floating particles of detritus. The detritus is swallowed, the bacteria are digested, and the particles are passed back to the water where new layers of bacteria will form to nourish more animals. The essential role of the abundant bacteria is to continually decompose dead plants and animals and thus reduce their constituents to basic minerals—nitrates, phosphates, etc.—which provide the nutrient supply for a new cycle of plant life. There is a continuous loop.

This continuous removal of phytoplankton, zooplankton, and detritus into the food web is an effective method for storing the nutrients that flow through the estuary (page 32).

24

The life of the bottom, collectively termed the *benthos*, is typically more abundant in estuaries than in either fresh waters or the ocean. This bottom community is critical, not only for its yield of shellfish but also because it is a major element in ecosystem stability and supply of forage for sport and commercial fishes. The benthic species are highly diverse, including worms, lobsters, clams, oysters, shrimps and fishes. Many species forage about within the bottom sediments for their food. Others feed by filtering the water passing by.

The complexity of biotic systems emphasizes our earlier argument for the ecosystem approach in coastal management and reinforces the following basic Management Principle: *Each coastal ecosystem must be managed with respect to the relatedness of its parts and the unity of its whole.*

Patterns of Life

It is important to recognize that each species has a distinct life pattern and set of strategies upon which its survival depends. Different management actions may be required because of different dominant species, but the ecosystem has to be managed *as a whole system*. No piecemeal management of single components or single species will succeed.

The sort of fine tuning of environmental controls that is required must be done in the light of specific ecological knowledge. In each management program, the services of a professional ecologist or biologist will be required to inventory the biota of the particular locale and to reveal specific points of vulnerability of the numerous important species and the ecosystem as a whole. This information should become the basis for selection of environmental criteria to be used in planning and management. It will also suggest the particular land-use control measures (e.g., designation of *vital areas*) or performance standards (e.g., dredging limitations) needed to protect the species and the ecosystem.

Each species makes specific demands on its environment and the accumulated total of these demands gives the ecosystem its particular biotic character. For example, the spotted weakfish, with its mottled pattern of coloring, is perfectly camouflaged for safety from predators so long as it lives among the submerged grasses of the Florida estuaries. If the grass beds were to be killed by sedimentation, the weakfish would have no place to hide and would succumb to predators or leave the area. Besides, the spotted weakfish depends for its nourishment on the grass shrimp and small fish that occupy grass beds.

It is not possible to review here details of the life patterns of the hundreds of valuable and interesting species of birds, fish, shellfish, mammals, and plants that inhabit the coastal ecosystems. But in the next section we do discuss some especially vulnerable estuarine dependent species.

Estuarine Dependence

Of hundreds of species of coastal fishes, the most important for commerce and sport are often the migratory species that depend on estuaries to fulfill special needs for certain of their life functions. Walford *et al* have summarized this as follows:[20]

> One group of migrant Atlantic fishes spends summer in the estuaries and winter off-shore in deep waters; for example, croaker (hardhead) and spot (lafayette) do this. Others, such as the winter flounder, prefer deeper waters in summer and spend winters in the estuaries. Anadromous species such as salmon, shad, alewife (river herring) and striped bass come in from the ocean to go up the rivers for spawning. Catadromous species, such as the eel, live in fresh and brackish waters but spawn in the sea—but the young return to the estuaries and to fresh waters.

A few important fish, such as the white perch, and spotted sea trout, reside permanently within the protected waters. Some migratory sea fish, such as weakfish, redfish, mullet, and black drum, spawn inside the protected waters of the estuary. In total, some 60-70 percent of Atlantic and Gulf Coast species of fish are estuarine dependent.[12] However, few Pacific Coast fish species are estuarine-dependent. Some important shellfish are also involved in estuarine dependence patterns. As examples, two estuarine dependent species, shrimps and striped bass, are discussed below.

Shrimps are found along all U.S. coasts. Many are commercially useful and all are essential to the food web. The peneid shrimps of the South Atlantic and Gulf Coasts (the brown, pink and white) are the most valuable commercially (Figure 17). The diet of various species appears to consist of plant detritus and small crustaceans, worms, and various larvae. Although most species are oceanic residents as adults, the estuary fulfills two primary functions for certain life stages of these shrimps: (1) provision of adequate nourishment during a period of rapid physical growth and (2) protection from predators.

The pink shrimp, abundant in the Gulf of Mexico, spawns offshore in water 100 to 150 feet deep. The larvae move and drift with currents toward the mainland for three to five weeks while passing through a series of developmental stages and growing to a size of about ½ inch. They enter the inlets and within the estuary they grow rapidly, reaching

26

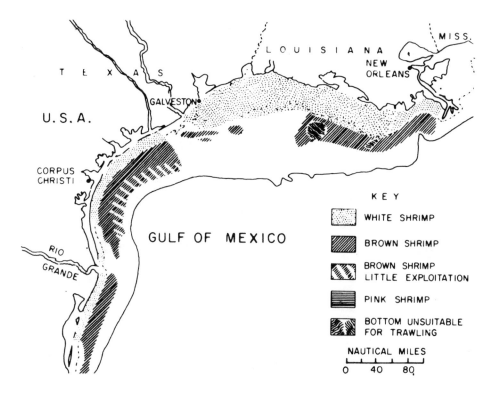

Figure 17. Shrimping areas of the western Gulf of Mexico (after Hilderbrand).[21]

commercial size in two to four months before returning to the sea to complete their life cycle (Figure 18). The closely related brown shrimp spawns offshore in depths of 150 to 230 feet. The young move inshore to remain for several weeks in the estuary. The other important Gulf of Mexico species, the white shrimp, inhabits water less than 100 feet deep and has a life cycle similar to the brown shrimp although it resembles the pink shrimp in having a greater affinity for fresh water.[21]

Striped bass occur on the Atlantic Coast from northern Florida to Canada, most abundantly from North Carolina to Massachusetts. Pacific striped bass are most abundant in the San Francisco Bay system, but some occur north to Oregon.

Stripers live in bays, sounds, and tidal rivers (in the Middle and North Atlantic coasts), depending on season. Few go more than four to five miles from shore. At their southern or northern extremes, Atlantic stripers seem to be wholly river fish. In the Middle Atlantic, populations divide their year between ocean and estuarine feeding and wintering

27

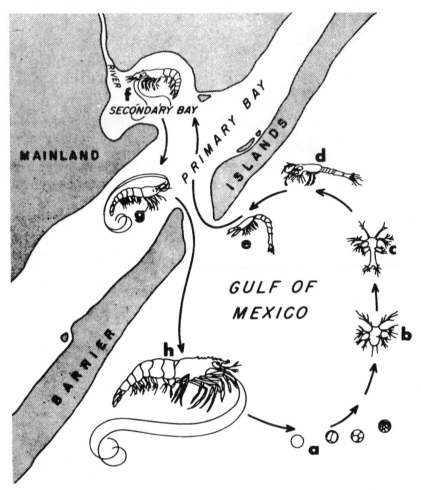

Figure 18. Typical life history of the Gulf of Mexico shrimp: (a) shrimp eggs, (b) nauplius larva, (c) zoea, (d) mysis, (e) postmysis, (f) juvenile shrimp, (g) adolescent shrimp, (h) adult shrimp.[3]

grounds and riverine spawning grounds. Distances traveled grow progressively longer with age. Stripers feed on a variety of prey found near shore, including fish, crabs, worms and shrimp.

Striped bass breed along the Atlantic Coast as far north as the Hudson, but not successfully in New England rivers. They spawn in fresh or nearly fresh water of tidal rivers from April through June.[22] Their life patterns—a long pelagic larval life, congregation of small fish on shoals, winter hibernation in deeper water, summer dispersion, coastal migration —demonstrate the remarkable compatibility of the striped bass and the

28

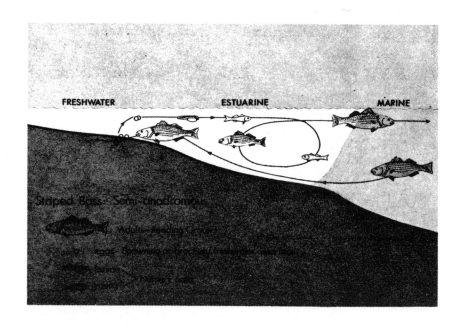

FRESHWATER   ESTUARINE   MARINE

Striped Bass: Semi-anadromous

Figure 19. Life cycle of the striped bass.[10]

estuary (Figure 19).

Striped bass introduced in the San Francisco Bay region in 1879 bred successfully and flourished there. Like the Atlantic populations, they spawn in the spring and summer. Spawning occurs principally in the Sacramento and San Joaquin Rivers and, to a lesser extent, may occur in rivers tributary to certain Oregon estuaries. As in the Atlantic, the young are waterborne for many weeks then settle down to life in the upper estuary. They move toward bays as they grow older. Abundance of striped bass had decreased to nearly half of the previous level by the 1960's, which may be owed to entrainment of suspended stages in water diversions and power plants.[23]

The essential point in the above discussion is how necessary the estuarine system is to the survival of coastal migratory species. Without close study one might not even link such species as bluefish, mackerel or channel bass to estuaries, or realize how very dependent the early lives of menhaden, striped bass and croaker are upon safe and healthy conditions in the brackish tidal rivers. It is clear that management programs must include an element for protection of migratory species with complex life histories, particularly those that are linked to estuaries where the effects of pollution and other disturbances can be so especially damaging to their life support systems. Management for such species is complex

29

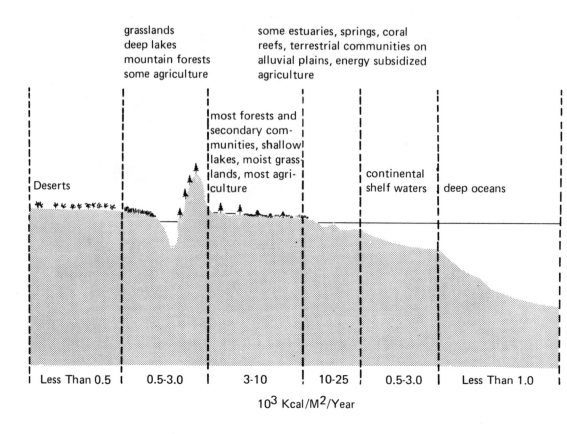

Figure 20. The world distribution of primary production in terms of annual gross production (in thousands of kilocalories per square meter) of major ecosystem types. Only a relatively small part of the biosphere is naturally fertile. (From E. P. Odum.) [1]

because it requires coordination of programs between communities and between states.

ECOLOGICAL CONCEPTS

One finds within the subject matter of ecology several concepts that relate to management of coastal ecosystems. They provide a framework for understanding how organisms survive and interact with the forces and conditions of their environment. The following discussion serves to explain the more important of these concepts.

Productivity

The concept of *primary productivity* refers to the capacity of an ecosystem to produce basic plant material. Technically, primary productivity

30

is the amount of energy converted from light, nutrients and carbon dioxide to plant tissues within a unit of area during a unit of time; for example, the grams of carbon fixed per square meter per day. In terms of primary productivity, estuarine water bodies may produce 20 times as much as the deep sea and 10 times as much as either nearshore waters or deep lakes (Figure 20). Since primary productivity governs the ecosystem's total capacity for life, estuaries are generally more productive than the ocean.

Productivity measures are useful to ecologists in understanding the sources of energy that fuel an ecosystem. They are also useful in diagnosing the condition of an ecosystem because they are a measure of the potential capacity to support life. By comparing *actual* abundance of life with the *potential* abundance, one can determine if the system is malfunctioning and needs attention.

Energy and the Food Web

Energy needs of coastal ecosystems are met in two ways: (1) from external driving forces, and (2) from internal supplies that are recycled within the system. The major external driving forces of coastal ecosystems are tide, ocean currents, river inflow, wind, sunlight and the basic inorganic nutrients (minerals) that nourish plants and animals. The appropriate Ecological Principle is: *The flow and amount of available energy governs life processes within the coastal ecosystem.*

Internally, the chain of life—food chain or food web—begins with energy assimilated by plants. Plants, the producers, use the energy of sunlight in photosynthesis to transform carbon dioxide and basic nutrients into plant tissue, a form of energy which is available to animals as their basic foodstuff. The plants are then eaten and passed through the complex food web and back to basic nutrients (page 18). Because all animal food starts with plants, every organism ultimately depends on the major factors that limit the building of plant tissues, such as: the supply of basic nutrients, the amount of carbon dioxide available and access to sunlight.

A detailed energy flow analysis requires highly specialized skills because the systems are so complex—as shown in Figure 21—and may not be a practicable option for many management programs. However, a general knowledge of energy flow is useful in choosing criteria for certain elements of a coastal management program, such as: (1) water clarity, (2) aquatic vegetation, (3) nutrients and (4) water flow.

The following are two examples of considerations that should be addressed in management: (1) water clarity—control silt from land

31

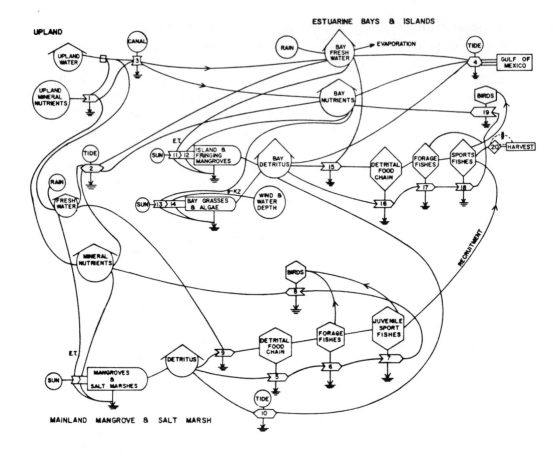

Figure 21. Estuarine ecosystem model.[11]

erosion which blocks sunlight penetration to aquatic plants beneath the
water surface and (2) aquatic vegetation—prevent the utilization of
marshes to prevent loss of marsh grass acreage. In both of these examples,
the management purpose is to maintain the energy subsystem which
converts sunlight to basic animal food.

These considerations lead to the following Management Principle: *To
maintain an ecosystem at optimum function it is necessary to protect and
optimize the sources and the flows of the energy that power the system.*

Storage

Storage capacity is an exceptionally important aspect of the coastal
ecosystem. *Storage* is the capability of a system to store energy supplies
in one or more of its components. Such a storage unit can be a stand of
marsh grass, a fish school, a seed, organic sediment on the bottom or

32

phytoplankton in the water of a bay. These units all gather and store a supply of energy which is a reserve against shortages.

Storage in plant tissues is particularly important because the reserve of nutrients stabilizes the system and provides a buffer against irregular heavy stresses or seasonal shortage periods (winter). Storage is nature's hedge against boom-or-bust fluctuations of abundance and scarcity, according to the following Ecologic Principle: *A high capability for energy storage provides for optimum ecosystem function.*

Estuarine vegetation is particularly important as a storage unit. For example, marsh grass in its entirety—roots, leaves, flowers, stems—provides storage upon which the regularity of nutrient supply to the estuarine food chain depends. In addition, marshes have vast quantities of nutrient stored in their soils which provide an always available source of nourishment to the marsh grasses, as explained below for the Georgia marshes:[13]

> Fertilizing nutrients are absorbed in the mud and are present in sufficient reserve to last for 500 years without renewal. Renewal, however, is going on continuously. Grasses remove nutrients from the mud, down to a depth of several feet, but nutrients are reabsorbed into the mud again as water percolates through burrows and cracks. The standing stock of grass, both living and dead, contains a large reserve of nutrients, in the sense of fertilizer, and potential foodstuff for everything from bacteria to large fishes. Because the grass decomposes slowly throughout the year, there is a constant and quite even supply of materials. The result is a productive and stable ecosystem.

There is an urgent need to understand the value of storage because *storage components may appear as ecologic largesse* and thus are easy victims of development. The value of storage leads to an important Management Principle: *Storage components of ecosystems are of extreme value and should always be fully protected.*

In addition to the living components of the system the storage protection principle also applies to nonbiotic components of the environment which serve important ecological functions. For example, sand dunes are, above all, a giant storehouse of sand that function to resupply and stabilize beach fronts periodically torn away by violent storms.

Succession

The ecological concept of *succession* refers to a sequence of species replacements in a particular area. It is used to describe the changes in biota that occur either over extended time because of long term changes

Figure 22. An ecotone is a biologically rich transition zone between distinct natural communities such as these marsh-forest and tideflat-marsh boundaries.

in environmental conditions, or those that occur rapidly because an area has been disturbed suddenly. In management, one is most concerned with succession that follows on a sudden change, either man-made or natural. An example of succession following man-made disturbance is the replacement of grasses by shrubs, and then by trees, when wetlands are converted to drylands by filling. An example of succession following a sudden natural event is the following sequence found on barrier beaches when bare sand is suddenly exposed by storms—sand, sparse grass, closed grass canopy, shrub savanna, closed shrub canopy, forest. The final equilibrium plant community is known as the *climax state*.

Diversity

Diversity expresses the variety of species present in an ecosystem. It is generally assumed that a high diversity of species leads to better ecosystem balance and provides a greater resilience to catastrophic events, such as disease. Conversely, a low diversity may indicate a stressed system or one that has been degraded, for example, by pollution. Ecologists have used the *diversity index* as a measure of the condition of an ecosystem *vis-a-vis* potential adverse impacts. Lowered diversity (fewer species) indicates that environmental disturbances have upset the ecosystem.

Ecotone

An *ecotone* is the transition area at the edge or border between two different communities, as between a marsh and a forest (Figure 22). Ecotones combine the characteristics of the communities they separate and, while limited in size, they often have an unusually high abundance and diversity of life and serve a unique function to the ecosystem.

Carrying Capacity and Standing Crop

Carrying capacity is the limit to the amount of life that can be supported by any given habitat in number or mass. The term may refer to the number of individuals of a particular species or of all species—but always as a *potential*. The *actual* number (or mass) of species present in an area at any one time is the *standing crop*. Thus, in the ecological sense, carrying capacity is the ultimate constraint imposed on the biota by existing environmental limits, such as the availability of food, space or breeding sites, or by disease or predator cycles, temperature, sunlight or salinity. The carrying capacity of a system can be markedly reduced by man-made disturbances that reduce available energy supplies or energy utilization

The term carrying capacity is often used in a more general, non-ecological, sense; for example, as an expression of the total resource capability of an area. In addition, the term has found use in social and economic sciences. Therefore, it is always important to understand the specific context in which the term is used.

Indicator Species

An *indicator species* is one chosen to represent conditions in an ecosystem because it is either especially sensitive to change in the environ-

35

ment or because it is a particularly easy-to-work-with indicator of eco-system condition. An indicator species may be used in management to monitor the effects of pollution or other degradation of an environment by comparing the present standing crop of a species to the standing crop during a previous undisturbed condition, or to some specified standard. Certain invertebrate species of the bottom are preferred indicators because they stay in place and because they are sensitive to disturbances. The pitfalls of this method of monitoring lie in sampling errors and in the difficulty of ascribing an observed change to a specific type of disturbance; for example, toxicity compared to nutrient reduction.

CHAPTER 2

Environmental Disturbance

Development activity anywhere in coastal areas—watersheds, flood-plains, wetlands, tidelands or water basins—is a potential source of ecologic damage to the coastal waters ecosystem. Each type of urban, commercial or industrial development has the potential for a particular combination of environmental disturbances (see Chapter 4). The amount of damage that may result from any disturbance depends upon the characteristics and vulnerabilities of the specific ecosystem involved.

Often the same qualities that make a coastal ecosystem so valuable also make it vulnerable to damage from pollution and other environmental disturbance. This is particularly true for estuarine ecosystems. Estuaries, surrounded by land on all sides, are easily accessible for urban or industrial development and for water-related human uses. Use pressures are heavy in urban areas adjacent to estuaries and the pollution potential is high. The confinement and shallowness of estuarine water basins allows pollutants to pervade their waters, particularly those that have poor flushing characteristics. Although estuarine water is in motion because of tidal action, the resultant flow may be mostly reciprocal, rather than directional, and the process of discharge to the ocean slow in non-stratified estuaries. Conversely, the subsurface landward flow of a stratified estuary may propel pollutants suspended in the lower layer toward the productive upper estuary.

In this chapter we describe certain basic constraints on shoreland development. We also discuss the effects of the major types of disturbance and the impacts to be expected from each, in light of known ecological properties of coastal waters. We propose a general plan of impact assessment along with recommended criteria for monitoring the condition of the ecosystem or for setting performance standards on development activities.

SHORELANDS

The connection between shorelands and coastal water components of the coastal ecosystem is primarily through the flow of water. Therefore, a main management consideration for shorelands is control of the quantity and quality of runoff to coastal waters.

One must start with the presumption that shoreland development will have adverse effects on coastal ecosystems by modifying runoff patterns and thereby reduce the capability of the land to both store and regularize the release of rainwater (or snow and ice melt) from the watershed, and to cleanse it enroute to coastal waters. Clearing the land of vegetation has many effects. One is a decrease in the watershed's ability to hold back storm waters. Another is an increase in the total volume of fresh water delivered to the estuary caused by one or both of these factors: (1) a lesser fraction is transpired to the atmosphere because there is less vegetation, and (2) a lesser fraction is evaporated to the atmosphere because the water moves to rivers faster over cleared land.

Other alterations in flow may be caused by water control activities— such as storage (dams and impoundments) or diversion from the watershed for agricultural, domestic or industrial use (Figure 23). Covering the land with impervious surfaces and installation of storm drain systems unbalances flow patterns and delivery schedules and prevents recharge of ground water aquifers.

Diversion of water from the watershed, channelizing rivers or clearing and surfacing of land may result in reductions of sources of dissolved nutrients to coastal waters or cause the inflow to move so quickly to sea that the ecosystem is deprived of needed nutrients. The basic Management Rule is: *Reduction of the natural supply of nutrients to the coastal ecosystem by alteration of fresh water inflow is unacceptable.*

Uncontrolled construction activities greatly increase the amount of sediments, nutrients and other substances, including a wide variety of contaminants, carried down to estuaries with the fresh water runoff. The appropriate Management Rule is: *Any significant discharge of suspended solids, nutrients, or toxic chemicals is to be presumed adverse and is unacceptable.*

After development is complete, continuing water quality problems may result from fertilizers and biocides applied to the landscape (page 113) and from the discharge of industrial and domestic wastes.

The discipline of hydrology, as it applies to the land surface, is well advanced and its principles should be familiar to planners, water engineers and ecologists. We can apply these same principles to management of coastal ecosystems to explain the factors that control land sources of water so important in their influence on coastal water systems. It is a particularly important management practice to maintain the flows of water in and to the ecosystem so that the natural salinity regime is

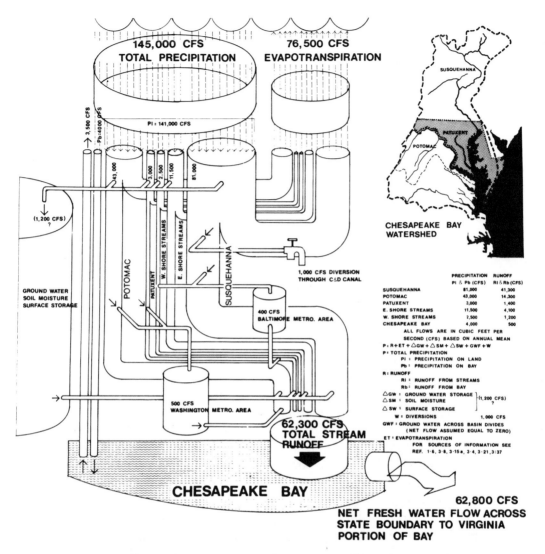

Figure 23. Chesapeake Bay water budget.[24]

maintained. The appropriate Management Rule is: *Any significant change from the natural salinity regime is presumed ecologically detrimental and is unacceptable.*

On the presumption that a desired goal is for the ecosystem to continue to function optimally, there are to be specific constraints on project location, design and construction activity throughout coastal watersheds. The amount of impervious surface is to be minimized. Barren soils are to be stabilized by replanting vegetative cover as quickly as possible

39

after land clearing. Finished grades are to be designed so as to direct waterflows along natural drainage courses and through natural terrain where the vegetation can cleanse runoff waters. Conventional storm drain systems are to be eliminated whenever possible in favor of non-structural, natural-type land drainage systems with grades that direct runoff flow through vegetated drainage courses. Where natural-type systems are not feasible, structural storm drain systems are to be designed to harmonize with natural drainage patterns, to preserve the natural rate of flow, and to provide for release of effluents into *buffer areas*, vegetated shoreland zones, for natural purification.

Channeled Flow

Included in channeled flow are all permanent and temporary rivers, streams and creeks, along with all intermittently flooded drainageways—sloughs, swales and so forth—which convey land runoff toward coastal waters. If the coastal ecosystem is to be maintained at optimal function, all of these conduits are to be left in their natural state. This leads to the following Management Rule: *Alteration of any drainageway by re-alignment, bulkheading, filling, impounding or any other process that shortcuts the natural rate or pattern of flow or blocks or impedes its passage is unacceptable.*

A buffer area of sufficient width is required between the edges of each drainageway and the surrounding developed land to cleanse runoff water and to stabilize its rate of passage overland. Without such buffers the water tends to surge into the channels too rapidly and lacks the exposure to vegetation required to purify it. The buffer strip includes at the minimum the complete floodway of each channel—both floodway and floodway fringes (Figure 24).

Depending upon the amount of intended development in a watershed area, additional width must be provided to offset the progressive effects of runoff contamination and unbalancing of rates and periodicity of runoff associated with increasing development. This leads to a basic Management Principle: *The higher the degree of development, the greater is the need to provide vegetative buffer area along drainageways.*

Surface Flow

Except for certain flat lands, like the Florida Everglades, surface flow occurs only intermittently following rainfall. Problems with contamination of coastal waters from urban runoff typically start with surface flow over paved areas and other impervious surfaces. The best strategy for preserving the normal hydrologic regime is to permit this runoff water

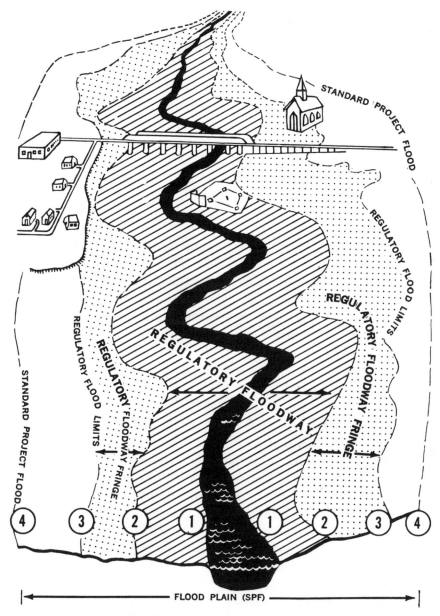

1. REGULATORY FLOODWAY—Kept open to carry floodwater—no building or fill.
2. REGULATORY FLOODWAY FRINGE—Use permitted if protected by fill, flood proofed or otherwise protected.
3. REGULATORY FLOOD LIMIT—Based on technical study—outer limit of the floodway fringe.
4. STANDARD PROJECT FLOOD (SPF) LIMIT—Area subject to possible flooding by very large floods.

Figure 24. Riverine flood hazard areas.[25]

41

to flow through vegetation in order to stabilize its flow, to provide for natural removal of contaminants and to enable it to percolate into the ground. This can be accomplished by appropriate land grading to control surface water and to divert its flow through natural vegetated drainage-ways. Suitable buffer strips along the coastal shoreline provide for scrubbing of non-channeled surface flow that runs directly to coastal water basins. In respect to any land surface in the shorelands, it must be presumed that the natural pattern of drainage is the most favorable to the coastal ecosystem. This leads to the basic Management Principle: *A fundamental goal of shoreland management is to retain the system of land drainage as near to the natural pattern as possible.*

Subsurface Flow

The soil has a large capacity for water storage when its surface is open; it can then serve as a primary flow stabilizer. Underground water moves very slowly down to coastal waters, allowing time for removal of pollutants by natural purification. The benefit of this natural process is enhanced by minimizing any interference with the infiltration of water into the soil, such as occurs when the surface is covered with impervious materials. Drainage canals are especially detrimental because they short-circuit ground water flow by intercepting it and carrying it rapidly down to the coastal water basin.

COASTAL WATERS AND BASINS

Of the various factors that govern the response of coastal ecosystems to environmental disturbance, perhaps the most important is the circulation of water in the water basin. Circulation characteristics control the kind and intensity of land use to be permitted in the adjacent shorelands. Patterns of circulation and form of water basin can be categorized into several basic types to assist in the management program.

In this section we discuss and categorize different circulation properties of estuarine and ocean ecosystems. We also describe certain constraints on land and water use that are required by the natural characteristics of the different ecosystem types.

A basic Management Rule concerning water is: *Any significant change from the natural rate of water flows of a coastal water basin is presumed to be ecologically detrimental and is unacceptable.*

Circulation Types

Each of the four major coastal water circulation types described below is controlled by a different combination of tide, fresh water inflow and oceanic currents. These types are somewhat arbitrary and therefore most useful for planning reconnaisance. Management programs will often require specific studies by appropriate experts of the patterns of each water body—the details of flow pattern, velocity, flushing rate and so forth.

1. *Oceanic circulation*

The oceanic circulation type is characterized by vigorous currents, waves, and tides that sweep away and dilute contaminants of land origin. These forces cause sandy beachfronts to shift about and to remain unstable and generally unsuitable for building.

Oceanic circulation is ordinarily less complex than estuarine circulation except in areas near inlets. But inlet areas are most often to be considered estuarine in character and for most management purposes treated as estuaries.

One complexity of importance is coastal *upwelling*, a common occurrence along much of the ocean front where bottom water moves *inshore* to replace surface water pushed *offshore* by prevailing winds. One effect of this is that contaminants discharged to the ocean may be carried directly back onshore by this bottom current.

The management implication of the typically active oceanic circulation type is that the water itself is less susceptible to degradation from discharge of contaminants, because water motion greatly reduces their chance for accumulation and, usually, pollution concentrations are more quickly dispersed than in estuarine water basins.

2. *Stratified estuarine circulation*

The typical estuarine water body is layered or stratified, with fresh water moving seaward at the surface and saltier water moving inland at the bottom (page 14). Under favorable conditions these layers move at sufficient speed to provide good circulation throughout much of the stratified estuary. The velocity of flow and the volume transported both decrease toward the fresh water section of the river. Higher fresh water flows induce both higher surface outflow and bottom inflow. Also, the strength of these flows governs the position of the *salt front* and therefore the location and abundance of fish and microorganisms.

The accumulation, concentration and dispersal of pollutants is a function of the combined rates of flow of these two layers. Generally, the typical stratified estuary is less vulnerable to pollution than its opposite, the mixed or unstratified type, because flushing of pollutants is more rapid. However, the bottom flow can recycle pollutants that sink, sending them inward to the upper estuary.

3. *Non-stratified estuarine circulation*

In the mixed or non-stratified type of estuary, water movement is weaker and the flushing rate is lower than in the stratified type. Still, there may be sufficient circulation from fresh water flow and tidal action. The flushing characteristics will depend upon the combination of these two factors. Specific professional study of the individual water body should precede management actions.

Mixed estuaries are generally more vulnerable to pollution than stratified estuaries but are less vulnerable than lagoons.

4. *Lagunal estuarine circulation*

Lagunal type circulation is characterized by poor water movement resulting from: (1) a lack of significant fresh water input to the lagoon and (2) a lack of strong tidal exchange because of the typical restricted size of inlets connecting the lagoon to the sea. Wind is often the main force driving circulation.

The severe use limitations appropriate to this circulation type are set forth in the next section (page 47).

Water Basin Types

Coastal water basins occur in a nearly limitless variety of shapes, sizes, depths and appearances. The six water basin types discussed below will cover most cases. Specific management programs will usually require the assistance of an ecologist to provide a detailed understanding of the particular water basin involved.

1. *Exposed coast*

Exposed ocean shorefronts pose different management problems than the shores of the various types of estuaries. The ocean shorefront is characterized by either solid rock formations or by heavy deposits of sand. These shorefronts are rugged—they receive the full brunt of ocean storms. They do not have delicate and easily damaged tidal areas like the marshes of confined waters.

Figure 25. The Cape Cod National Seashore, Cape Cod, Mass.

Sand beaches are tough and resilient (Figure 25). They require little management attention other than to prohibit any removal of sand. In contrast, the dunes lying just behind the beaches are fragile, easily damaged and require the most extensive safeguards. Their great capacity for storage of sand makes them the chief stabilizer of the ocean beachfront. When the dunes are damaged so that they erode away, the essential buffer is gone and the whole shore is threatened with each winter storm or hurricane (page 74).

2. *Sheltered coast*

In certain places along the ocean shorefront where the bottom slopes gradually away from the shore, offshore sandbars are thrown up by the force of waves. Similarly, coral reefs often build up in a barrier formation seaward of the shorefront. These sand or coral barriers provide a sheltered area inside the bar or reef where the ecosystem is in many ways characteristic of confined waters—marine grasses grow, shellfish prosper and nursery areas for young fishes are found. In addition, there are "low-energy" coasts (such as the northwest Florida shore), where wave action is so reduced that, even without a bar in front, the coast is sheltered in character. In all sheltered coast areas, water movement is reduced and the effects of pollution are much increased compared to waters of open ocean coasts. These sheltered coasts are to be managed separately from exposed coast systems. Management needs are similar to those of embayments.

3. Bay

Bays are the larger confined coastal water bodies (here including sounds). Many water bodies are misnamed as "bays"; they are really embayments or lagoons and should be so categorized in the system proposed here. Because bays are typically quite open to the sea and receive strong tidal flow, bays are flushed more effectively than embayments or lagoons. The flushing action is augmented by river discharge, particularly when stratification is pronounced. Bays vary greatly in size and in type of shorefront. Management needs are similar to those of lagoons and embayments but controls usually can be somewhat less restrictive.

4. Embayment

Embayments are confined coastal water bodies with narrow restricted inlets and with significant fresh water inflow. They have more restricted inlets than bays and are generally smaller and shallower. Embayments usually have low tidal action and since the fresh water inflow is often not an adequate substitute, they may be easily polluted and filled with sediment.

Management programs for embayments require controls nearly as restrictive as those for lagoons, except for those embayments characterized by unusually high rates of flushing. The vulnerability of the embayment is related to its size—the smaller ones are more vulnerable and require more severe restrictions for equivalent inlet width and fresh water flow.

5. *Tidal river*

A tidal river is the lower reach of a coastal river. The coastal water segment extends from the sea or estuary into which the river discharges, to a point as far upstream as there is significant salt content in the water, the *salt front*. (The tidally influenced fresh water part is excluded.) Tidal rivers may be well flushed by the combined action of tide and fresh water outflow. The pollution damage potential varies in severity depending upon the degree of flushing and other natural factors. The tidal river basin may be a simple channel or a complex of tributaries, small associated embayments, marshfronts, tidal flats and so forth. It should be managed as part of the bay or embayment into which it discharges.

6. *Lagoon*

Confined coastal water bodies with restricted inlets to the sea and without significant fresh water inflow are termed lagoons. It follows that they have very limited circulation of water, are poorly flushed and therefore relatively stagnant. Because of this, pollutants may easily build up and become pervasive in lagoons. Sediment accumulation is rapid in lagoons and shoaling of the basin potentially great. The shores are often gently sloping and marshy; they are ecologically valuable and also vulnerable.

The aquatic communities of lagoons may be quite different from those of other basins because of physical differences in a higher and relatively constant salinity, somewhat less extreme temperatures, a somewhat higher and more constant pH and a greater effect of wind.

In management programs, lagoons need a maximum of protective controls. These controls may include: wide buffer strips above wetlands; no direct discharge of septic tank, sewage plant or storm drain effluents; maximum safeguards against runoff of fertilizers, biocides, soils and so forth; and restrictions on industrial activity. Boat traffic may have to be controlled to prevent turbidity from agitation of sediments, damage to grass beds and boat pollution. Generally the size of the lagoon dictates the severity of controls, smaller lagoons requiring the most extensive restrictions.

IMPACT ASSESSMENT

In planning for coastal land and water-use management, it is necessary to identify, through impact assessment, the ecosystem hazards associated with specific types of utilization. Some types of use involve project construction which would lead to gross *disturbance* of the ecosystem or would endanger or preempt unique or critical habitats. Certain other uses would have potential adverse disturbances from project operation lasting for the duration of their existence.

Advance study, including prediction of environmental impacts and exploration for alternative development solutions, is a requirement of law (the National Environment Policy Act of 1969) for land or water development enterprises that involve the Federal government. Also, many states now have legal requirements for environmental review of certain development project types. At the center of the impact assessment idea is a *presumption of adverse effects* for certain identified development programs. The term *adverse effect* may be defined as follows: [26] "Effects are considered adverse if environmental change or stress causes some biotic population or nonviable resource to be less safe, less healthy, less abundant, less productive, less aesthetically or culturally pleasing, as applicable; or if the change or stress reduces the diversity and variety of individual choice, the standard of living or the extent of sharing of life's amenities; or if the change or stress tends to lower the quality of renewable resources or to impair the recycling of depletable resources."

The concept of impact consideration has spread beyond statutory requirements into the environmental consciousness of society at large.

Whether it is called "environmental impact," "impact evaluation," "environmental effects analysis" or any other similar term, the concept is the same. We use the term *impact assessment*—by which we mean the evaluation of adverse and positive ecological effects and the determination of their impact on human needs.

In impact assessment it often appears desirable to focus concern on *important species* rather than the whole system. One must be cautious of this selection though, because it would be easy to ignore certain species that are not appreciated as being important to the continued functioning of the ecosystem. By one definition: "A species, whether animal or plant, is 'important' if it is commercially or recreationally valuable, if it is rare or endangered, if it is of specific scientific interest or it is necessary to the well-being of some significant species (e.g., a food chain component) or to the balance of the ecological system." [26]

One component of a management program should be an impact prediction system which would have the specific purpose of determining

48

the probability of significant adverse impact from any particular type of project or activity. The system should also address the possibility that environmental improvement might result from certain projects, although the likelihood of *net* benefit may be quite low.

It is possible to predict such ecologic disturbances as: change in flow rate, loss of tideland vegetation or sediment, thermal, nutrient, or toxic substance discharge. It also is possible to assess the consequences of such disturbances to the ecosystem but difficult to quantify them. An analysis of these factors through environmental impact assessment is useful in determining necessary constraints on the siting and design of coastal development projects.

A great variety of methods have been devised to assess the cause-and-effect linkage of human activity and environmental harm. We have taken the essential elements which these methods share and melded them into a system of impact assessment that is useful for the purposes of coastal land-use planning and management.

Impact Cycle

Impact assessment is the study of a cycle of events, linked in a chain of causes and effects, that proceed from human needs. These needs lead to specific *projects*, which can be categorized under broader *programs*. If a project leads to an environmental disturbance from some activity it sets off a series of ecological *effects*. If these effects degrade the ecosystem, they cause an *environmental impact* which detracts from human needs. In short, man's projects often backfire through the ecosystem. We are only now learning the wisdom of accurately predicting the long-term environmental impact of our activities.

The impact chart depicted in Figure 26 shows how one can break down the cycle of causes and effects into a workable series of elements. These are defined as follows:

> *Human needs:* The state of tension between what mankind has and what mankind wishes to have.
> *Program:* A broad initiative taken to fulfill some human need or needs (housing, agriculture, etc.).
> *Project:* One specific action taken under a program (housing subdivision, new farm, etc.).
> *Construction activity:* An individual process involved in the construction of a project facility, mostly short-term effects.
> *Operation activity:* An individual process in the operation of a project, long-term effects.

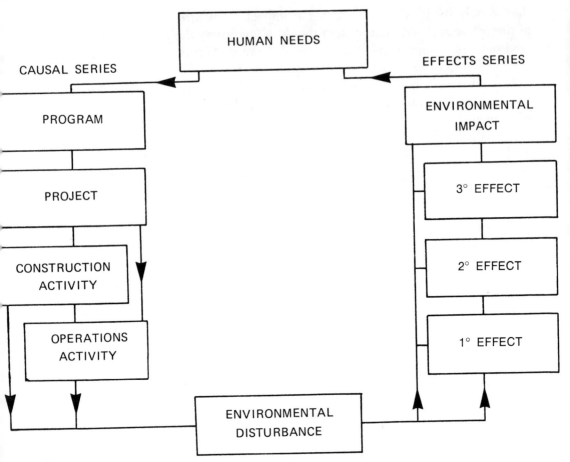

Figure 26. The impact cycle describes the pathways of cause and effect leading from development activities through ecosystem disturbances to detrimental impacts.

> *Disturbance:* A disruption of an ecosystem, a perturbation.
> *Ecologic effect:* The reaction of an ecosystem to a disturbance.
> *Environmental impact:* An environmental change that affects the fulfillment of a human need. Adverse environmental impacts lead to social detriments.

This arrangement is man-centered. It is designed to accommodate the normal philosophy of management which relates to the needs of mankind and to describe that pattern of events which results in predictable negative effects on the welfare of mankind. One can rightfully make the argument that an impact is adverse if it degrades an ecosystem without any linkage back to mankind. However, we find it useful to "close the loop" and to construe *effects* as the consequences to the ecosystem and *impact* as the consequences to the present or potential (future) needs of mankind.

The *causal series* of the impact cycle is sequential except that programs which cause disturbances do not always have a significant construction stage, for example, agriculture or logging. This case is shown by the causal pathway leading directly from project to continuing activity. Conversely, some programs lead to projects that cause a major disturbance in the construction phase but not afterwards, for example, estuarine installation of a submerged pipe.

The *effect series* is made up of a number of effects that proceed from one to another, that interact, feedback and so forth. For simplicity we have shown only three stages of effects in Figure 26. At times the linkage may be very involved. At times it is so simple that the whole effects series is shortcircuited; for example, land clearing (construction) may lead directly to intense fresh water dilution of an estuary from rapid storm water runoff (disturbance) and cause a mass death of edible clams (environmental impact) that cannot survive the freshened water. Here the adverse impact, or detriment to mankind, is the loss of the clam resource.

The Disturbance Web

Usually the sequence of effects between disturbance and impact is more in the likeness of a web than a chain, because of interactions and feedbacks. Often a profusion of effects leads directly from a single disturbance. Conversely, a number of separate disturbances may lead to a single effect. A typical array of effects is illustrated in Figure 27, where projects which require dredging are used as an example of activities that result in a complicated pattern of disturbances and effects.

Analysis and comprehension of this complex type of pattern—a difficult task even for a knowledgeable scientist—may be required to solve certain management problems. However, much of the routine work of planning and ecosystem management can proceed at a simpler level. Where the more complex situations arise, it is important to recognize that detailed assessment of environmental impact is work for professional ecologists, although they will often need the assistance of engineers and others.

The Impact Matrix

The matrix chart is a tool sometimes used in impact reconnaissance, although it is of little use in case assessments because it relates only a

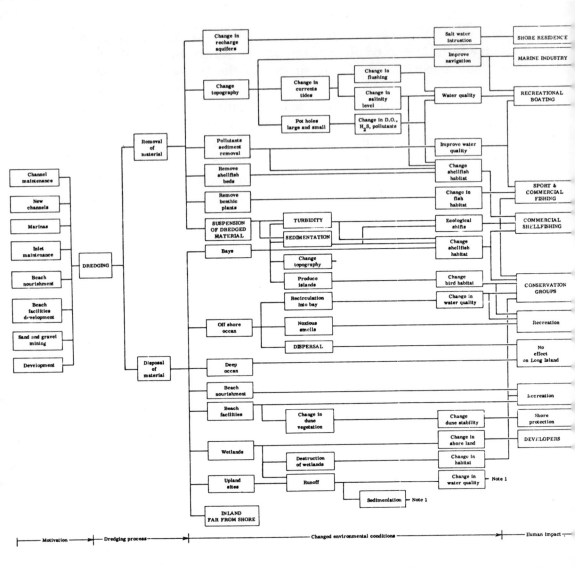

Figure 27. A typical effects linkage shows the disturbance web and environmental impacts of dredging.[21]

single pair of variables and does not explain: the mode of action of effects, the complex patterns of interaction or, usually, the scale or magnitude of inputs. Its purpose is to provide a checklist, an analytical framework, or an organizing tool.

An example of a matrix display is given in Figure 28, which lists the possible disturbances resulting from known project construction or operations activities. A somewhat more sophisticated approach might include

52

ENVIRONMENTAL EVENTS \ POSSIBLE USE RESTRICTIONS	1. Aesthetics	2. Commercial Fishing	3. Mining	4. Mariculture	5. Transportation	6. Utilities	7. Recreation	8. Residential Construction	9. Preservation of Fish & Wildlife
1. BOD		●		●			●		●
2. Dissolved Oxygen		●		●			●		●
3. Nutrients		●		●			●		●
4. Pathogens		●		●			●		●
5. Floatables	●	●		●	●		●		●
6. Odors and Tastes	●	●		●			●		●
7. Color	●	●		●			●		●
8. Toxicity		●		●			●		●
9. Dissolved Salts		●	●	●			●		●
10. Suspended Solids	●	●		●			●		●
11. Radiological		●		●			●		●
12. Temperature		●		●		●	●		●
13. Ph Buffering		●	●	●			●		●
14. Ground Water				●					●

(Row group label: WATER QUALITY)

Figure 28. Matrix that relates selected human activities and water quality effects—dots in cells identify interactions (adapted from ref. 28).

an evaluation system consisting of index numbers in each cell of the matrix which would indicate the seriousness of the effect, say on a scale of 1 to 10.

ECOSYSTEM CONDITION

Since the object of a coastal land and water environmental management program is to maintain the quality of the coastal ecosystem, it is

53

useful to regularly measure and monitor the quality of the ecosystem. While a complete program of monitoring may be feasible only for advanced management programs, some of the simpler tests can be used in even the most basic programs. The condition index also finds use in setting *performance standards*—specific requirements for control of ecologically disturbing activity. Most available data sources concern water quality and sources of pollution.

Water pollution is largely controlled by a complex program of joint Federal and state laws. Among other aspects, this program implements water quality standards prescribed by the U.S. Environmental Protection Agency (EPA) under Federal regulation.[29] Aside from their use in pollution control enforcement, these standards make a useful set of guidelines for: (1) local monitoring of ecosystem condition and (2) establishment of enforceable performance standards. They provide an index to the success of coastal land and water management programs that function in synchrony with the machinery of pollution control. Quantitative standards are most applicable to routine programs, but there are also some qualitative criteria that have a place in monitoring.

Quantitative Criteria

The quantitative EPA coastal water quality standards are discussed below along with supplementary comments of our own.

Toxic substances: The maximum allowable concentrations of toxic substances as established by the EPA,[15] following a National Academy of Sciences review in 1973,[30] are summarized in Tables 2 and 3.

Pathogens: EPA 1973 standards for pathogenic organisms in swimming waters essentially prohibit concentrations higher than a log mean of 200 fecal coliforms per 100 ml. of water. In non-swimming waters the standards essentially permit concentrations to an average of 2000 per 100 ml. (There are no standards for viruses or other pathogens.)

Oxygen: EPA 1973 standards require that dissolved oxygen concentrations be maintained at 6.0 ppm, or higher. The standard recognizes that natural phenomena may cause the concentration to fall as low as 4.0 ppm.

Temperature: EPA 1973 standards limit artificially induced increases in temperature to not more than 1.5°F in summer —June through August—or more than 4.0°F during the rest of the year.

54

Table 2. Coastal Water Quality Criteria for Toxic Substances Other Than Biocides. Source: U.S. Environmental Protection Agency [15] and National Academy of Sciences.[30]

SUBSTANCE	Maximum Acceptable Concentrations (96 hr LC$_{50}$) [1] [2]	Maximum Acceptable Concentrations (Milligrams or Micrograms/liter) [2]	Minimum Risk Threshold (Milligrams or Micrograms/liter) [3]
Aluminum	1/100	1.5 mg/l.	0.2 mg/l.
Antimony	1/50	0.2 mg/l.	N.A. [4]
Arsenic	1/100	0.05 mg/l.	0.01 mg/l.
Barium	1/20	1.0 mg/l.	0.5 mg/l.
Beryllium	1/100	1.5 mg/l.	0.1 mg/l.
Bismuth	N.A.	N.A.	N.A.
Boron	1/10	N.A.	5.0 mg/l.
Bromine[5]	N.A.		N.A.
Cadmium[6]	1/100	0.01 mg/l.	0.2 ug/l.
Chromium[7]	1/100	0.1 mg/l.	0.05 mg/l.
Copper	1/100	0.05 mg/l.	0.01 mg/l.
Fluorides	1/10	1.5 mg/l.	0.5 mg/l.
Iron	N.A.	0.3 mg/l.	0.05 mg/l.
Lead[7]	1/50	0.05 mg/l.	0.01 mg/l.
Manganese	1/50	0.1 mg/l.	0.02 mg/l.
Mercury[8]	1/100	1.0 ug/l.	N.A.
Molybdenum	1/20	N.A.	N.A.
Nickel	1/50	0.1 mg/l.	0.002 mg/l.
Phosphorus	1/100	0.1 ug/l.	N.A.
Selenium	1/100	0.01 mg/l	0.005 mg/l.
Silver	1/20	0.5 ug/l.	N.A.
Thallium[9]		0.1 mg/l.	0.05 mg/l.
Uranium	1/100	0.5 mg/l.	0.1 mg/l.
Vanadium	1/20	N.A.	N.A.
Zinc	1/100	0.1 mg/l.	0.02 mg/l.
Cyanides[10]	1/10	0.01 mg/l.	0.005 mg/l.
Detergents	1/20	0.2 mg/l.	N.A.
Phenolics	1/20	0.1 mg/l.	N.A.
Phthalate Esters	N.A.	0.3 ug/l.	N.A.
PCBs[11]	N.A.	0.002 ug/l.[12]	N.A.
Sulfides[13]	1/10[12]	0.01 mg/l.[12]	0.005 mg/l.[12]

[1]The maximum acceptable concentration figures in this column are expressed as fractions of the 96 hr. LC$_{50}$ for the most sensitive species in a given area. The 96 hr. LC$_{50}$ is that concentration of a substance which kills 50 percent of the test species within 96 hours under standard bioassay conditions.
[2]Data are Environmental Protection Agency official criteria where

available; National Academy of Sciences data used where EPA data not available.

[3]National Academy of Sciences data, for concentrations "below which there is a minimal risk of deleterious effects."

[4]N.A.—adequate data not available.

[5]The maximum acceptable concentration for free (molecular) bromine is 0.1 mg/l, for ionic bromate, 100 mg/l.

[6]In the presence of copper or zinc in concentrations of 1 mg/l or more, the minimum risk threshold should be lower by a factor of 10.

[7]In oyster growing areas, the minimum risk threshold should be lower.

[8]According to the National Academy of Sciences, "Fish-eating birds should be protected if mercury levels in fish do not exceed 0.5 mg/g. Since the recommendation of 0.5 mg/g in fish provides little or no safety margin for fish-eating wildlife (birds), it is recommended that the safety of the 0.5 mg/g level be reevaluated as soon as possible."

[9]1/20 of the 20-day LC_{50}.

[10]Marine and estuarine acquatic and wildlife criteria not available; fresh water criteria are used (by EPA).

[11]According to the Environmental Protection Agency: "The maximum acceptable concentrations of PCB in any sample consisting of a homogenate of 25 or more whole fish of any species that is consumed by fish-eating birds and mammals, within the size range consumed is 0.5 mg/kg on a net weight basis."

[12]Data supplied by National Academy of Sciences.

[13]These concentrations are valid only if salt water pH is between 6.5-8.5.

Table 3. Coastal Water Quality Criteria for Manufactured Biocides. Recommended Maximum Concentrations of Biocides in Whole (Unfiltered) Water Sampled at any Time and any Place, in Micrograms/Liter. Source: U.S. Environmental Protection Agency.[15]

Organochlorine Pesticides

Aldrin[1]	0.01	Endrin[1]	0.002
DDT[2]	0.002	Heptachlor[1]	0.01
DDE[2]	0.006	Lindane[2]	0.02
Dieldrin[1]	0.005	Methoxychlor[2]	0.005
Chlordane[2]	0.04	Toxaphene[2]	0.01
Endosulfan[2]	0.003		

Organophosphate Insecticides

Azinphosmethyl	0.001	Fenthion	0.006
Ciodrin	0.1	Malathion	0.008
Coumaphos	0.001	Mevinphos	0.002
Diazinon	0.009	Naled	0.004
Dichlorvos	0.001	Oxydemeton Methyl	0.4
Dioxathion	0.09	Parathion	0.0004
Disulfonton	0.05	Phosphamidon	0.03
Dursban	0.001	TEPP	0.4
Ethion	0.02	Trichlorophon	0.002
EPN	0.06		

Carbamate Insecticides

Carbaryl	0.02	Zectran	0.1

Herbicides, Fungicides and Defoliants

Aminotriazole	300.0	Diuron	1.6
Dalapon	110.0	2–4, D (BEE)	4.0
Dicamba	200.0	Fenac (Sodium salt)	45.0
Dichlobenil	37.0	Silvex (BEE)	2.5
Dichlone	0.2	Silvex (PGBE)	2.0
Diquat	0.5	Simazine	10.0

Botanicals

Allethrin	0.002	Rotenone	10.0
Pyrethrum	0.01		

1 and 2Maximum acceptable concentration in any sample consisting of a homogenate of 25 or more whole fish of any species that is consumed by fish-eating birds and mammals, within the size consumed on a net weight basis, expressed as ug/kg (EPA data available only for organochlorine pesticides). Note 1: 5 ug/kg. Note 2: 50 ug/kg.

Qualitative Criteria

The following are useful qualitative criteria for which there is not a basis for quantitative standards:

Nutrients: No standards are available to limit nutrients that cause eutrophication, but earlier EPA criteria (1968)[31] recommended prevention of any releases that cause enrichment leading to any major change in the natural levels of flora (attached or floating plants, including phytoplankton). (Tight controls on nutrients are required in estuaries where the eutrophication potential is high.)

Circulation: The 1968 EPA criteria recommend that there be no activity permitted which would change basin geometry or fresh water inflow such that the ecosystem is adversely affected.[31] (To this we would add a similar restraint on any interbasin transfer of incompatible estuarine waters.)

Turbidity: The 1968 EPA criteria recommend no discharge of substances that will result in turbidity levels that are deleterious to biota.[31] Also they state that turbidity levels less than a Secchi disc reading of 1 meter (3 feet) or equivalent in Jackson Turbidity Units (JTU) "shall be regarded with suspicion." (Certain states prohibit turbidity *increases* exceeding 50 JTU above natural levels.)

Salinity: The 1968 EPA criteria recommend that no alteration in channels, basin geometry or fresh water inflow be allowed that would cause a permanent change of more than 10 percent greater or lesser salinity than the existing *natural* level.[31] (These are important criteria but difficult to implement because they require determining the effects of: (1) water flow far upstream in the fresh water sections of the rivers and their watersheds, (2) dredging to improve navigation and (3) significant alterations of circulation caused by structures or modification of the bottom or shoreline of water basins.)

Sedimentation: No specific standards are available. (Any detectable shoaling of a water body is cause for vigorous management efforts to eliminate soil discharge, dredging, land erosion or other source.)

Habitat: No specific standards are available on tolerable losses of habitat. (Any loss of habitat must be presumed adverse, not only of fixed and obvious entities such as coral reefs or grass beds, but other important habitats such as tideflats or certain submerged bottoms as well.)

Productivity: No standards are available for primary productivity. (A loss of productivity is to be presumed adverse. For monitoring, rather accurate checks can be made on the crops of rooted plants, but plankton production is difficult to measure.)

Fauna: No standards are available. (The best indicator of ecosystem quality may be the life itself—the abundance and diversity of species—any significant reduction of which is to be considered adverse, as is any shift in biotic communities from desirable to less desirable species. However, accurate quantitative sampling of aquatic fauna is a difficult art even for experts and usually may not be relied upon to accurately register small changes in abundance.)

CHAPTER 3

Resource Evaluation and Protection

A management program created to protect and sustain a coastal ecosystem must be compatible with ecologic theory. Furthermore, it must be tailored to the specific qualities of the ecosystem to be managed.

The essential qualities of a coastal ecosystem can be segregated into three categories—features, processes and characteristics. The *features* are the fixed physical objects, such as coral reefs, mud flats or grass beds. *Processes* are the driving forces of the system; such as, sunlight, water flow or nutrient recycling. *Characteristics* are the variable qualities that give each ecosystem its distinctiveness, such as the species mix, the temperature or chemical content of the water. Analysis of these factors is useful in evaluation of ecosystems providing the procedure is not so complex as to obstruct its basic purpose—the design and execution of an effective management program. A system of evaluation and classification is required that can simplify the nearly limitless complexities of nature.

Standard ecologic classification does not readily provide a useful management framework. One can, however, work with ecologic concepts and generally known relationships to devise a practicable system—one that recognizes differences in capability for use imposed by variations in landscape and waterscape and relates these to specific management options and actions.

In this Chapter we advance the idea of identification of *vital areas*, components of such importance to the functioning of the system that they must be preserved as intact units and given special protection from adverse influences. The *vital areas* are related to a broader system of resource capability designation that classifies all shorelands and coastal waters for *preservation, conservation,* or *development.* Finally, a method for resource designation and for mapping coastal areas is suggested.

VITAL AREAS

There are many components of the coastal ecosystem that are of such importance to certain species or to the functioning of the entire ecosystem as to require that they be classified as *vital areas* and provided (1) im-

59

munity from virtually all types of use and (2) protection from pollution and other external sources of disturbance. The protective program will involve both control of water use within the boundaries and abatement of pollution of water that flows across the boundaries from outside.

A *vital area* most often would be a *fixed* ecosystem feature of tangible physical character, such as a submerged oyster bed or a cordgrass marsh. Fixed vital areas are readily located, surveyed and mapped, and remain constant in location. However, there are many *transient* features of the water mass which have specific attributes but not fixed boundaries that need a high degree of protection. An example of a transient *vital area* is the salinity controlled feeding area for young white perch, which may shift up or down the estuary 10 miles or more in response to river inflow (the zooplankton food of the perch lives within a restricted salinity).

Transient *vital areas* change location but their boundaries shift between known limits and therefore it is possible to map out bounds which normally will encompass the full area, say 95 percent of the time. Such limits will be suitable for management purposes.

Fixed *vital areas* are readily evaluated, surveyed and mapped, and will remain virtually constant in location. They should not be dug or dredged out, filled over, or otherwise obliterated or altered.

The remainder of this section is devoted to description of certain important types of *vital areas*, the ecologic functions they perform, and their major vulnerabilities to environmental disturbance.

Coral Reefs

Coral is a living organism. As coral colonies grow they build reefs which are not only uniquely rich and beautiful but also highly sensitive to environmental disturbances. A much higher degree of protection than has been practiced in the past is necessary to preserve these *vital areas*. Sediment discharge from erosion, sewage pollution, chemical pollution and urban runoff all must be strictly controlled where reefs are significantly influenced by land drainage. Dredging in the vicinity of reefs may be particularly harmful because of the high incidence of silt fallout and sunlight screening caused by turbidity (Figure 29).

The following impacts have been noted by coral reef expert, R. E. Johannes:[32]

> Suspended sediments, which reduce light penetration, inhibit coral growth. Sediments settling on corals may kill them within a few days if the blanket is thick enough. The planktonic larvae of corals and many other reef invertebrates cannot settle and colonize soft shifting sedi-

Figure 29. Silt from turbid or muddy waters caused by dredge and fill operations smothers and kills coral reefs.[33]

ments. Dredging and coastal land filling associated with harbors, marinas, ship channels, etc., and sand removal for construction and beach replenishment has injured or destroyed hundreds of reef communities. Sewage is probably the second worst form of pollution stress on reef communities (through accelerated effects of eutrophication and oxygen in tropic ecosystems and overgrowth of algae which can smother corals). Another stress due to bad land management—accelerated runoff of freshwater—has sometimes lowered coastal salinities to the point where shallow reef communities have been completely killed within a few hours. Thermal effluent from power plants has killed corals and associated organisms in Florida, Hawaii, The Virgin Islands, Guam and elsewhere.

Johannes believes that under proper controls the collection of shells, corals and aquarium fishes could be permitted but that research to provide the basis for these controls is lacking. In the absence of contrary proof, it must be concluded that any reduction of a coral reef structure decreases its function as a marine habitat, its scenic quality, and its role as a natural breakwater. Therefore, it is recommended that removal of reef materials for commercial purposes should not be permitted and that amateur collection of coral by swimmers and divers be prohibited.

61

Kelpbeds

Kelpbeds are an especially important component of certain coastal ecosystems, especially those of the partially sheltered waters off rocky Pacific shores. Kelp grows best in relatively cool waters with rich bottoms and depths of less than 100 feet. Kelp provides food and favorable habitat for many fishes, as well as sheltered vital nursery areas for their young (Figure 30). Stands of kelp are a favored haunt of sea otters and other marine mammals. The kelpbed breaks the force of the sea and provides a strip of quieter water between it and the shore, an effect which benefits many additional forms of shorelife.

Management plans should include protection of kelp against significant environmental disturbances. Sewage discharges may be adverse to kelp because the water enrichment favors the food chain of sea urchins and they in turn eat the kelp. Other potential dangers are chemical and thermal pollution and damage from boat propellers. Whether the harvest of kelp to produce algin and other saleable compounds should be allowed is a matter of unsettled controversy in California.

Shellfish Beds

Clams, oysters, and other valuable shellfish are not spread evenly over the bottom of estuaries but rather they are to be found concentrated in certain flats, banks, bars or reefs (Figure 31). These shellfish beds are *vital areas* that are rather easily identified and delineated in planning surveys.

Shellfish are notorious for filtering out of the water such harmful substances as bacteria, pesticides and toxic metals and concentrating them in their tissues, thus exposing the animals or people that eat them to dangerous concentrations. For this reason, millions of acres of estuarine shellfish beds have been closed to harvesting. A better solution than closing beds is to control the sources of pollution. This will not only make the shellfish safe, but maintain the natural balance of the ecosystem.

Many ecosystem disturbances are harmful to shellfish. For example, silt-laden waters are a harsh environment for their planktonic young stages and layers of mud make an unsuitable bottom for most of them—even a thin veneer of silt over otherwise clean surfaces prevents oyster larvae from attaching. Fresh water deluges from carelessly developed watersheds may cause massive kills or damage to clam beds.

Grass Beds

Beds of submerged marine grasses are essential elements of the estuarine ecosystem, particularly in systems where marshes are reduced

62

Figure 30. Drawing of a representative kelpbed of the San Diego region.[34]

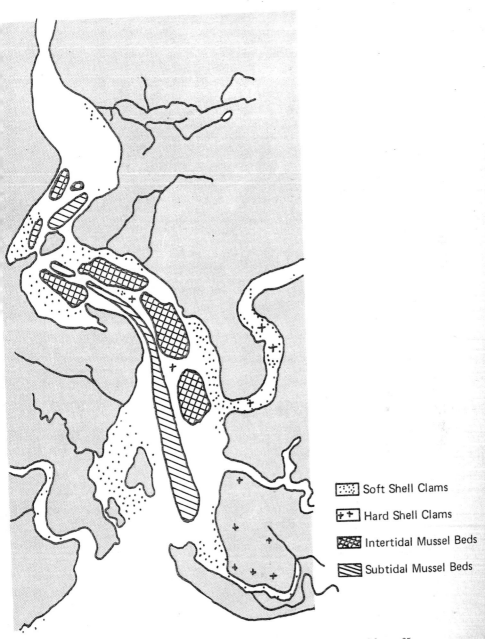

Figure 31. Major shellfish areas of the North River, Mass.[35]

- [::::] Soft Shell Clams
- [+ +] Hard Shell Clams
- [▨] Intertidal Mussel Beds
- [▨] Subtidal Mussel Beds

or absent (Figure 32). They often provide a substantial amount of the primary productivity and of nursery ground habitat available in estuarine waters.

Figure 32. Submerged grass bed community, St. John Island, U.S. Virgin Islands.

Marine grasses grow in shallow waters in all latitudes where the currents are not too swift, wave action is low and the bottom sediments are favorable. They prosper in the quiet, protected waters of healthy estuaries. Although the species of grass may differ from region to region, grass beds provide an ecosystem component of special value wherever they occur. They supply food to grazing animals, detrital nutrient to the water, add oxygen (during daylight hours), and stabilize bottom sediments. They provide *nursery areas* (vital places of refuge for young fishes and other aquatic life forms. They attract a diverse and prolific biota and often create unique opportunities for the existence of certain species. For example, the tiny larval stages of estuarine scallops must attach to grass blades to survive and, therefore, the species can exist only where there are grasses.

Eelgrass is the predominant submerged grass in the temperate estuaries, including most of the Pacific Coast and the Atlantic Coast to Virginia. Another species common in temperate areas is widgeon grass. In the

South Atlantic and Gulf of Mexico areas other species dominate, such as turtle grass or Cuban shoal weed.

In certain estuaries, marine grass beds are potentially as productive of detrital nutrient as salt marshes. For example, in South Oyster Bay, Long Island, eelgrass grows in waters six to eight feet in depth and covers about 60 percent of the bottom of the bay, in stands of 1-6 tons per acre (dry-weight)—the densest stands hold up to 14 tons per acre.[36]

The sea grasses serve an important role in stabilizing the sediments in which they grow. They continue to collect and hold within their root structure the suspended particles that drop out as water slows in passing the bed. The grass bed itself may collect enough sediment to be significantly elevated toward the surface and therefore toward the source of light.[37]

Marine grass beds are easily depleted, being especially vulnerable to pollution of all types, including heat discharged from power plants and the turbidity induced by them.[37] Turbidity from silt and eutrophication screens out light and prevents growth of grass. Fine sediment (mud) often creates an unstable bottom condition in which the grasses cannot anchor their roots. Boat traffic over grass flats may compound the problem by stirring up the sediments and ripping up the plants.

Loss or degradation of grass bed areas is most detrimental to the ecologic health of an estuary. Conversely, there can be too much grass. In waters that are highly polluted from sewage or urban runoff, grasses may become overdense and a nuisance to boaters and fishermen as they break loose, and drift in clumps to the surface (as in Great South Bay, Long Island). Pollution control should solve the overgrowth problem.

In the absence of contrary evidence, it must be assumed that marine grasses are beneficial to the ecosystem and are to be protected.

Drainageways

Drainageways throughout the shorelands and coastal watersheds deliver runoff waters directly to the coastal ecosystem and therefore are a vital component. It is essential that they remain unaltered and protected in order to: (1) properly regulate the rate of runoff flow, (2) cleanse the runoff water by settling out suspended matter and (3) enable vegetative takeup of dissolved contaminants (page 40). All floodways, sloughs, swales or other drainageways throughout the coastal watershed should be identified and designated for preservation as *vital areas,* since their disruption is inimical to the quality of the estuarine ecosystem.

66

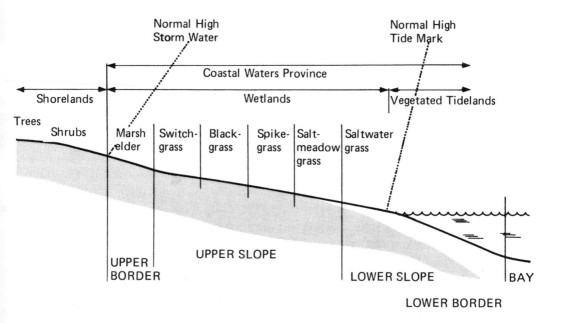

In addition to the typical sloped marsh shown above, we sometimes find depressions or ponds (called pannes) in tidal areas where tides flood occasionally and then water evaporates to create highly saline brine. This is where you will find glasswort, spikerush, sea lavender, and pink or purple gerardia. Although a spikegrass belt may occur, spikegrass is frequently found in a variety of wet sites.

Figure 33. Vegetative zonation of a typical southern New England shore (adapted from ref. 38).

Wetlands

In the profile of the coastal landscape, wetlands are the areas above mean high tide mark and below the yearly high storm mark (see Figure 55). They are naturally vegetated with wet-soil plants, usually salt tolerant types. They are part of the coastal water basin and their *inner* edge is the boundary between the coastal waters province and the shore-lands province (Figure 33). Immediately above the wetlands lie the floodplains. Below the wetlands lie the inter-tidal areas of the coastal regime: vegetated tidelands (salt marsh or mangrove swamp), bare flats, beaches or rock fronts. Wetlands are usually grass or rush meadows or marshes, but in tropical regions they may be vegetated with mangrove (usually black or white varieties). In the upper parts of some estuaries, salt water wetlands merge into fresh water wetlands.

67

Wetlands serve many of the same values as the vegetated tidelands in cleansing runoff waters and regulating their flow (page 70), and therefore they should be maintained as an essential component of the shoreline *buffer area* in developed areas. They serve, in the same manner as vegetated tidelands, to take up, convert, store and supply basic nutrient to the coastal ecosystem. Also, they provide essential habitat for certain coastal birds and animals. In addition, they absorb storm waters and help reduce coastal flooding to a degree.

While most experts agree that all existing vegetated tidelands—salt marsh and mangrove—should be preserved, they are not unanimous about wetlands preservation. It would appear that the value of wetlands in providing nutrient and habitat to aquatic species is normally lower than that of the vegetated tidelands. However, many experts may not appreciate their function in the hydrologic system—that they serve to regulate the flow of runoff waters and to cleanse them of contaminants. This role may be of major importance, particularly for areas undergoing heavy development in the shorelands.

Wetlands should be designated for preservation and protected from degradation by pollution, drainage channelization or other disturbances. They should not be preempted for highways or pipeline routes. Nor should their natural drainage be interrupted by canals or levees. After careful professional study of possible adverse effects they might be used for "polishing" of certain pre-treated waste effluents.

Vegetated tidelands

Paramount among the *vital areas* of many coastal ecosystems are the *vegetated tidelands*—salt marshes and mangrove swamps—common to estuarine shores of much of the U.S. coastal zone. Tidelands vegetation includes a wide range of salt-tolerant plants—the most prominent of which are grasses, mangroves and rushes (Figure 34). Included in this discussion are the intertidal areas only—the areas between the normal high water and low water marks. The wetlands (above normal high water) are discussed in the preceding part.

Vegetated tidelands serve as the vehicle for storage and transfer of nutrients from upland sources which are partially used and recycled within the tidelands system, but ultimately transported into the coastal waters to provide basic nutrient for the food web system (Figure 35). The vegetation plays a key role in converting inorganic compounds (nutrients) and sunlight into the stored energy of plant tissue. When the dead leaves and stems of the plants enter the water and are broken down by bacteria, they leave the storage component of the energy cycle

Figure 34. *Spartina* marshes are classified as *vital areas* because they are such highly productive components of estuarine ecosystems.

and, as small particles of organic detritus, they become the food of fiddler crabs, worms, snails, mussels and the myriads of larval stages of fish and shellfish of estuarine waters. About half the plant tissue created in vegetated tidelands (grass marshes and mangrove swamps) is flushed out into the estuary to support life there.[40]

The tidal creeks that transect vegetated tidelands provide a way for various fishes and invertebrates to move into the marshes to feed, to spawn or to seek sanctuary. Some species, such as the blue crab and various fishes, actively move in and out of these tide marshes while others, such as the copepods and the larvae of fish and invertebrates, are passively carried in and out on the tides.

Coastal areas with vegetated tidelands require special management consideration, not only to preserve the tidelands unit intact as a *vital area* but to control adverse land use practices in the floodplain and uplands above them. The vitality of a marsh or a mangrove swamp depends upon the quality and quantity of freshwater inflow that it receives from drainage of adjacent shorelands. The *natural* drainage pattern must be presumed to be beneficial, both in the manner by which waterborne nutrients are delivered to the estuary and the rate of the delivery. Development which accelerates runoff and channels discharge water

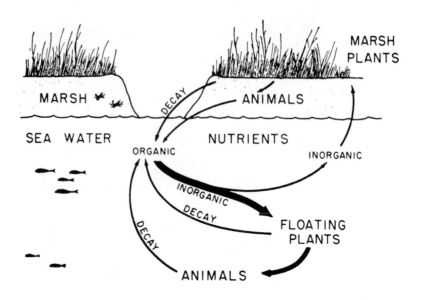

Figure 35. The marsh-estuarine nutrient exchange system.[39]

down drainage conduits may result in rapid sporadic flow that bypasses the marsh or mangrove swamp, carrying nutrients through the estuary too fast to yield their full benefit. Shoreland management can greatly reduce these adverse effects and even utilize the capacity of the tidelands vegetation to cleanse urban runoff.

Mangroves and marsh areas have the capacity to treat runoff waters and possibly, under careful controls, pretreated effluents may be polished within them. We have estimated from available information (in refs. 41, 42, and 43) that a marsh of 1,000 acres may be capable of purifying the nitrogenous wastes from a town of 20,000 or more people.

As it grows, tidelands vegetation also removes toxic materials and excess nutrients from estuarine waters. In addition, sediment and other inert suspended materials are mechanically and chemically removed from the water and deposited in the marsh or swamp reducing sedimentation of navigation channels and shellfish beds. The vegetation also slows the surge of flood waters and may help to reduce the severity of flooding.[44]

Intertidal vegetation serves to stabilize estuarine shorelines and prevent erosion. Mangrove trees not only preserve shorelines, but actually can extend the land's edge by trapping sediments and building seaward.[45]

It is quite possible to *plant* mangroves or marsh grasses along an altered shore to provide a buffer strip for stabilization and purification of runoff water (Figure 36).

Figure 36. A marsh grass buffer strip ten years after planting. Rappahanock River, Virginia (Interstate Commission on the Potomac River Basin).

Although vegetated tidelands can assimilate a reasonable amount of contaminants, they do have a limit and so must be protected from gross pollution from both land runoff and estuarine sources, and in particular from oil and toxic substances. A polluted marsh is offensive to the senses, while a healthy one is an aesthetic resource. Also, polluted marshes breed mosquitoes and other pests.

The pattern of drainage into the vegetated tidelands from the land is to be preserved in unaltered form for optimal ecosystem condition, as is the system of creeks that transects them and the existing pattern of tidal flushing (Figure 37). Tidal waters must have unrestricted entry to marshes and mangrove swamps. Such incursions as roads, canals, pipelines, drainage ditches and transmission lines are not to be permitted in

71

Figure 37. Aerial photograph showing the intricate drainage pattern of a salt marsh near Sapelo Island, Georgia (Note that marsh drains from the back side, away from the estuary).[46]

vegetated tidelands if the ecosystem is to function optimally. Such facilities should be built above the wetlands in the floodplain and adjacent uplands and designed so as not to significantly obstruct or impede runoff water flow.

In many ways the vegetated tidelands are not only a vital component of the estuarine ecosystem but of the human community which surrounds the estuary as well. The more intensely developed an area is, the more

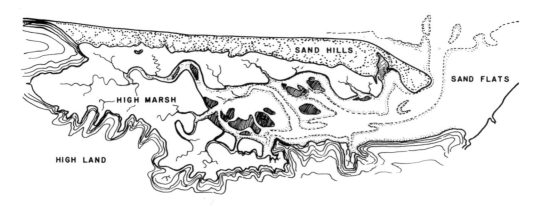

Figure 38. The Barnstable Marsh (Cape Cod, Mass.). Shaded areas are vegetated tidelands *(S. Alterniflora).*[47]

crucial the role of wetlands and the more urgent the need for their preservation through land use control.

Thus, the vegetated tidelands serve as an essential habitat, nutrient producer, water purifier, sediment trap, aesthetic attraction, storm barrier, shore stabilizer and, perhaps most important, as an energy storage unit for the ecosystem. It is obvious that as a coastal area becomes more occupied these benefits become more important. This applies to wetlands as well and leads to a single basic Management Principle: *The higher the degree of development, the greater is the need to preserve wetlands and vegetated tidelands.*

Tideflats

Tidelands are vegetated with grasses or mangroves to the mean low tide-line usually below which they extend into *tideflats*, areas exposed on low range tides as unvegetated expanses of mud or sand (Figure 38; also see Figure 22). These barren flats may extend above the mean low tide-line and thus create a tidal flat shoreline in tidelands unfavorable to growth of grasses because of heavy tidal scouring or other factors. Mudflats or sand flats are often rich sources of basic nutrients for the ecosystem and a feeding area for fishes at high tide or birds at low tide. In many estuaries they produce a high yield of shellfish or of baitworms for fishermen.

Tidal flats are often unappreciated because their values are not visible. When polluted they may become odorous and unattractive. Consequently, there is often community pressure to do away with them, but the potential for converting them to other uses is low.

73

Unless there is evidence suggesting that tideflats are not contributing significantly to the specific ecosystem in question, they should be protected as an integral and valuable part of the system. This protection of tideflats may be coupled with protection of the marshes behind them.

Dunes and Beachfronts

The beachfront is a harsh environment. Most animals that can withstand the high stress and constant motion of the beach sands are burrowing species—mole crabs, coquina clams, razor clams. Other species are temporary residents of the beach, such as sea turtles and the grunion fish that nest on the beach. Countless shore birds come to feed at the water's edge; the berm, sand dunes or sand overwash areas behind the beach serve as nesting grounds for many of them. The plant communities of the beachfront thrive on continuing natural disturbances and the plant species living here are especially adapted for the stress. The grasslands of the natural barrier island system perpetuated by overwashes are virtually the only natural grasslands in the eastern United States.[48]

Sandy ocean beaches are usually backed by sand dunes (Figure 39). A generally poor understanding of the capacity of the dunes to withstand alteration has frequently led to disastrous and expensive consequences. The following statement sets forth the basic characteristics and values of the dune system (adapted from a Conservation Foundation report by D. Frankenburg, L. Pomeroy, and others [13]):

> Dunes are waves of drifting sand, the height and movement of which is determined by the direction and intensity of the wind. The shifting dunes that normally lie directly behind the berm are the most subject to the stresses of wind and airborne salt. Mild summer waves add sand to the berm and prevailing onshore winds move it from the berm to the dunes. In winter and during storms the berm may be completely reclaimed by the ocean, at which time the dunes must erode to replenish the lost sand. The berm moderates these changes by providing a reservoir of sand available to either dunes or beach as needed.

> The dunes are greatly influenced by the presence or absence of the associated plant community. Most shifting dune plants (sea oats, for example) are rapid growers and spread by forming runners. An important function of the plants is to impede the rate of sand movement. Since prevailing winds are onshore, shifting dunes tend to move inland. Plants disrupt the smooth flow of air and allow

Figure 39. The ocean beach at Cape Hatteras, North Carolina. (By Joel Arrington for N. C. Dept. of Cons. and Dev.)

the sand to settle out on the front or top of the dune and it then does not move inland.

The fragile network of vegetation growing on shifting dunes is adapted to withstanding the rigors of wind, sand

and salt but not human feet, vehicles or grazing animals. When the mantle of vegetation is broken, the dune movement is accelerated to a point where plant growth can not keep pace with the shifting sand. The result is a chain reaction which leads to erosion and loss of the shifting frontal dune.

Behind the shifting dunes are the stable dunes, characterized by heavier vegetation—perennial shrubs, trees and vines. When prolonged drought, storms or hurricanes periodically erode the shifting dunes, the stable dunes absorb the brunt of the physical forces.

When both shifting and stable dunes are destroyed by man, there is nothing left to stabilize the remaining sea of drifting sand but man himself.

The great development pressure on dunes and sandy shorefronts often creates a difficult land use dilemma. These areas are most desirable locations for homes but they are at the same time environmentally sensitive and any development of them may set off a chain reaction of events creating large-scale problems. For example:

The destruction of buildings from tropical hurricanes and prolonged storms, from high seas and shifting sand, has occurred frequently in the past and will certainly occur in the future as long as people continue to build in dune areas. Even buildings on stable dunes are subject to periodic destruction, perhaps only once in fifty years.

Conflict between man and nature only reaches intransigent proportions after the buildings are in place and the erosion has begun to occur. Then the disaster funds are called in and the engineers attempt to stabilize with concrete and granite what the dunes achieved before, substituting sea walls for sea oats in the name of protecting human lives and property while further impairing the basic protective function of the sand dune system. What is so evident is that the trouble could have been avoided in the first place. Permanent structures should be placed in permanent places, behind the stable dunes where mature trees indicate a permanent environment.[13]

Because dunes and other features are easily destroyed by man's activities, there are many constraints on their use and that of surrounding floodplains and shoreland. In addition, potable water is often scarce and sewage disposal is difficult.[49] Vegetation must be kept intact and all

76

traffic, even foot traffic, must be prohibited altogether or strictly controlled. Highways are not to be built adjacent to mobile dune fronts. Holding the beach front in place by building protecting structures as substitutes for dunes requires Herculean effort and huge expense and usually is not permanently successful.

In summary, dunes are enormously valuable and exceptionally fragile. They should not be altered in any way. They are to be set aside for complete preservation and encompassed by as broad a buffer area as necessary to allow for their movement and to protect them and the larger system of which they are an integral part.

Barrier Islands

Much of the seacoast is fronted by elongate islands or peninsulas. These *barrier islands* are mobile features: they move and change in response to changes in sea level, currents, sediment supply and storms. These changes almost always involve patterns of erosion and deposition which constantly alter the shape and location of the islands. Stable ecology on the coastal islands depends first on the maintenance and perpetuation of the dune system. Dunes are not only the island's frontal defense against the forces of wind and waves (page 74), they are also the means by which islands move and grow.

On secondary dunelines—those lying landward of the frontal dune—there is a succession of vegetation that proceeds from grasses to forest communities and promotes large-scale trapping of sand whereby dune systems are stabilized and become rather permanent features of the landscape.

The ecosystem stability of the land and water areas behind the protective frontal line of dunes is dependent upon: (1) the dunes capacity to stop storm waves from cascading seawater across the terrain and (2) the dunes ability to hold the shore intact. While the beach itself is tough, the dunes are fragile and any alteration of them by removal of sand, construction on them, or traffic (even foot traffic) over them can lead to their demise.[49]

The following describes the ecology of the land behind the dunes on Georgia's barrier islands (adapted from reference 13):

Sheltered behind the last row of permanent dunes on the larger barrier islands are the forests which may cover most of the island (Figure 40). Ecologically beneficial forest fires are characteristically frequent and mild (slow burning ground fires) under natural conditions. Such fires do not ordinarily kill trees but merely burn the annual accumula-

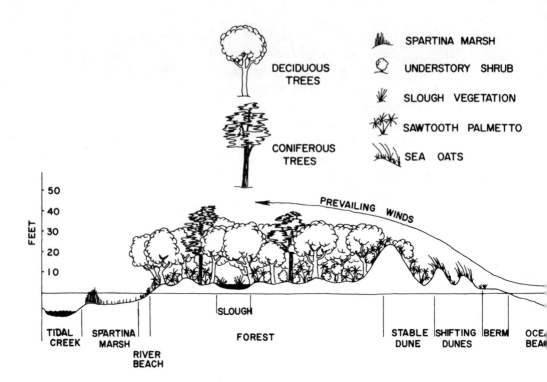

Figure 40. Hypothetical transect of a Georgia Coastal Island.[13]

tions of leaf litter while stimulating the growth of grasses and annual herbs.

Today, we extinguish these fires and island forests are becoming choked with dense underbrush and highly inflammable leaf litter. When fires do start, the litter burns hot, killing trees which take years to replace. Neither the dense underbrush nor the uncontrolled fires are favorable for native wildlife which ordinarily thrives on the grasses and insects associated with a fire-controlled ecosystem.

Water is a critical factor in the survival of island animals, and a variety of marshy sloughs provide for this need. Island sloughs can contain fresh or brackish water, range in area from a few square feet to many acres in extent, and be either permanent or temporary. They all have fluctuating water levels, the key to their high productivity and continued existence.

Dense island forest areas may be ecologically well suited for human use because the forest areas are protected from wind and waves and little

78

ecologic damage need result from construction of roads and buildings if proper constraints are invoked. But narrow or unforested islands are not capable of sustaining urbanization.

Barrier islands or peninsulas typically support marshes or mangrove swamps on the estuarine side. The values and characteristics of these vegetated tidelands are described in detail elsewhere (page 68). Briefly, marshes provide essential habitat for many forms of life and supply basic nutrient to the coastal ecosystem. They also stabilize the shore, absorb flood waters, and remove contaminants from the water. The vegetated tidelands are normally backed up by wetlands which serve similar functions. Both vegetated tidelands and wetlands are *vital areas* and require preservation and protection from degradation.

There are hazards connected with development of the floodplains of barrier islands, just as there are for the mainland (page 96). In addition, the whole barrier island or peninsula is classified as coastal watershed wherein all development is to be controlled to prevent adverse effects on the coastal ecosystem (page 37).

Typically protected by dunes on their ocean side and by vegetated tidelands and wetlands on their estuarine side, barrier islands may be so narrow that the two types of *vital areas*—dunes and vegetated tidelands— embrace most of their total area. Any natural sloughs and drainageways are also *vital areas*. The preservation requirements are such that little, if any, shoreland may be available for housing or other development on the narrowest barrier islands.

Breeding Areas

Many species which spread out for feeding concentrate in specifically defined estuarine areas for spawning. Often these areas are so limited in size that a major disturbance could lead to elimination of much of the spawning and to the virtual demise of the stock breeding there. It is necessary to conduct a specific survey to identify and locate spawning areas and to designate the critical ones as *vital areas*.

Breeding places vary from species to species. For example, salmon normally spawn only in specific shallow areas far up certain fresh water streams where the right gravels are present for the deposit of eggs. On the other hand, striped bass cast their eggs into the water of tidal rivers above the salt front so that the tiny hatchlings drift down into brackish estuarine areas (Figure 41). Winter flounder spawn mostly in deeper areas of the brackish upper ends of certain estuaries.

Some important species of waterfowl (e.g., mallards and wood duck) and most wading birds also breed in limited coastal locations. These areas are to be surveyed and set aside as *vital areas* with generous sur-

79

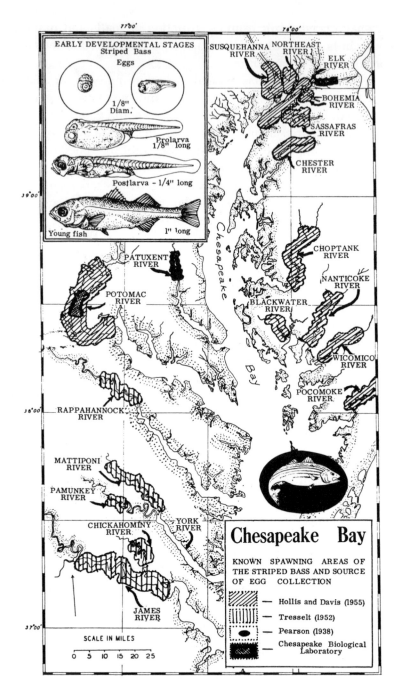

Figure 41. Range and location of spawning areas of striped bass in Chesapeake Bay, with illustrations of selected early development stages.[50]

80

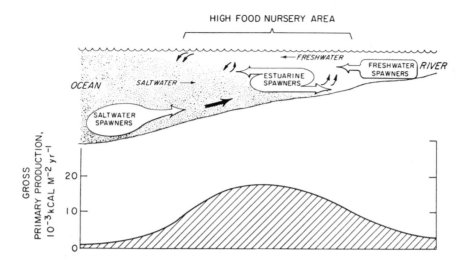

Figure 42. Productivity in various parts of a typical Atlantic estuary. (Adapted from Dovel.) [51]

rounding buffer strips to insulate them from the disturbances of human development and habitation.

Many seabird species breed in limited mainland *rookeries* or on isolated coastal islands. Seals also haul out for breeding at special coastal or island rookeries. All significant rookeries should be preserved intact and protected as *vital areas.*

It is common for young stages of coastal fish species to be planktonic; that is, to remain suspended and to drift with the currents for an extended period of time. In estuaries, this is a vulnerable stage of life and where there are special areas of concentrated drift of young, larval drift areas should be identified and provided status as *vital areas* so they may be protected.

Nursery Areas

The young of many coastal species settle into special areas called *nursery areas* when they are several weeks old. These are areas where the young creatures prosper because the right food is available, where predators are in the least abundance and where other conditions are most suitable for their survival (Figure 42). These precious nurseries are to be identified and mapped out as *vital areas* requiring a maximum of protection from environmental disturbance. They may or may not include within them other types of *vital areas,* such as marshes or tide flats. They may overlap with transient *vital areas* such as breeding areas or migration pathways.

81

A detailed survey of nursery areas is required in coastal planning because there is such a varied pattern of reproduction strategy among the various coastal species. For example, the young of striped bass drift down river into estuarine nursery areas (Figure 43). On the other hand, Gulf of Mexico shrimp spawn in the ocean, but the young move to estuarine waters after they are hatched to spend several critical weeks or months (see Figure 18).

Many primarily oceanic fishes are critically dependent on estuarine waters as nursery areas for their young. Like shrimp, these fishes—fluke, bluefish, menhaden, king whiting—spawn in the open sea (Figure 44). Their tiny young, after hatching, drift and swim shoreward, passing through the inlets where they find refuge and food in shallow estuarine waters. Some migratory oceanic fish—weakfish, redfish, mullet, and black drum—go inside the protected waters of the estuary to spawn. Their young grow up in the shallow nursery areas. A few important coastal fish are not oceanic migrants but live their whole lives within the estuaries; for example, the spotted sea trout of the South Atlantic. These year-round residents are completely dependent upon the estuaries for all their survival needs.

The nursery area pattern of oceanic spawning fish, very common for the Atlantic and Gulf of Mexico coasts, is less common for the Pacific where enclosed, warm and shallow waters are scarce. However, there are important Pacific anadromous fish (species that spawn in rivers but live in the sea as adults) like salmon, shad and striped bass as well as estuary-spawning fish like starry flounder whose nursery areas require protection as *vital areas*.

Wintering Areas

In northern latitudes, certain species cease feeding actively and retire to limited areas where they congregate for "hibernation". Where they concentrate in these special *wintering areas* the species are especially vulnerable to environmental disturbances. Such areas often require special protection from adverse effects, either by regulatory controls or by public acquisition (if there are lands involved).

As an example, most waterfowl species migrate from breeding places in the far north to concentrated winter areas in more southerly regions, the majority in marshes or shallow bays along Atlantic, Pacific and Gulf coasts (Figure 45). For example, two million ducks, geese, coots and swans winter on the salt marshes from New York to North Carolina.[126] All significant wintering areas for waterfowl require preservation and protection.

82

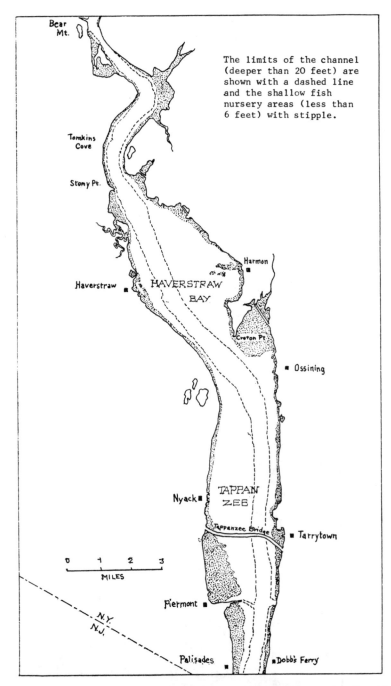

The limits of the channel (deeper than 20 feet) are shown with a dashed line and the shallow fish nursery areas (less than 6 feet) with stipple.

Figure 43. Primary shallow striped bass nursery areas in the Hudson Estuary, New York. Significant spawning areas are found from Stony Point north some 75 miles up the river valley.[52]

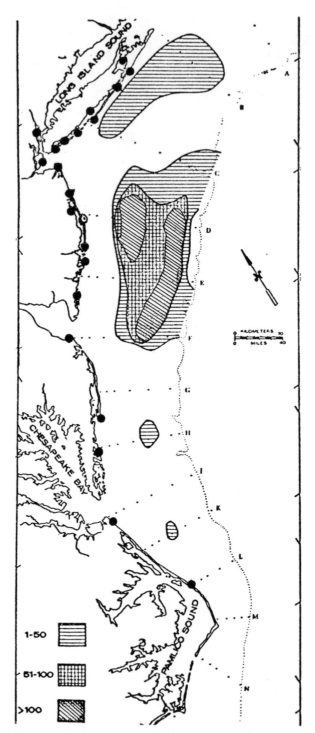

Figure 44. Offshore spawning areas of bluefish shown by shaded areas. Representative inshore nursery areas of bluefish shown by dots.[53]

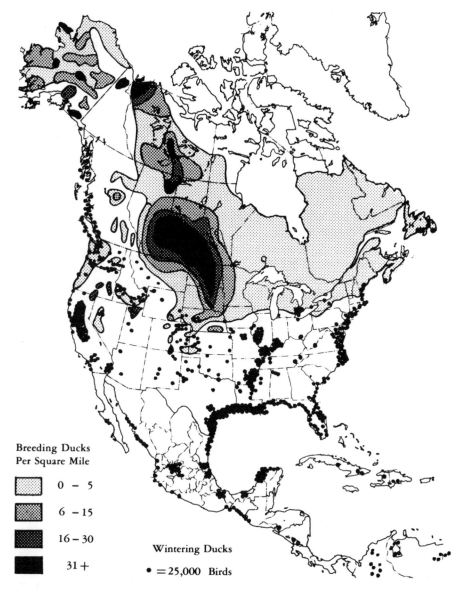

Breeding Ducks
Per Square Mile

	0 – 5
	6 – 15
	16 – 30
	31 +

Wintering Ducks

● = 25,000 Birds

Figure 45. Migratory ducks typically winter in certain places far to the south of their breeding areas.[54]

Fish, too, may have special wintering areas. For example, after spending the warm seasons feeding along hundreds of miles of seacoast, much of the northern population of Atlantic striped bass seeks refuge in freshened upper estuaries (tidal rivers) for winter. Here they are particularly vulnerable to many environmental dangers—toxic substances, power plant effluents and so forth (Figure 46). Some estuarine species

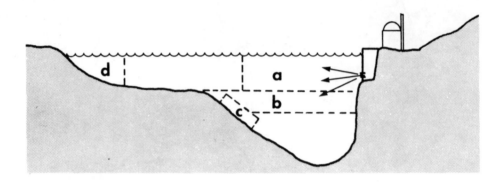

Figure 46. Profile of Hudson Estuary at the Indian Point Nuclear Power Station showing areas involved with specific functions of striped bass: a = migration pathway, b = juvenile wintering area, c = adult and adolescent wintering area, and d = nursery area (summer). Arrows indicate discharge of warm effluent that attracts juvenile fish to plant intake in winter where they are killed by suffocation against intake screens. (Adapted from ref. 55.)

spend the winter buried in specific parts of the bottom, where they can be destroyed by dredging activity or beset with bacterial infections acquired from polluted muds.

Feeding Areas

The feeding areas of mobile species are often quite circumscribed and may be located, mapped and preserved. Waterfowl have definite and readily definable feeding areas in sloughs or marshes and fishes may feed in certain areas, like shellfish beds, grass beds or coral reefs. These are ecosystem entities that are to be protected as *vital areas* for other reasons as well. But there are other not-so-well defined places that are restricted in extent and are important feeding areas, such as guts and passes or persistent tide rips where baitfish may gather to feed and gamefish come to prey on them (Figure 47), or shallow bottoms, rich in bottom fauna, where diving ducks forage. Any key areas of this type should be located, identified as *vital areas,* and provided protection from adverse environmental disturbances.

Migration Pathways

In their migrations, animals characteristically travel along specific restricted pathways. Flyways of birds may be identified visually, but the underwater pathways of fish are more difficult to locate. Fortunately these pathways are fixed by various physical properties of the environment

Figure 47. Coral reefs are biologically rich, beautiful and critically important *vital areas.*

and do remain essentially the same from year to year. *Anadromous* species (those that travel from the ocean to spawn in rivers) often migrate along well defined pathways—the shore edge, channel bottom and so forth. They can often be identified by an appropriate expert and set aside as *vital areas* for protection.

In a more general sense, most inlets from the ocean to estuaries (and often the channels between estuarine basins) are routes of migration of fishes, shrimps or crabs and should be safeguarded as *vital areas* where necessary (Figure 48).

RESOURCE CAPABILITY

The planning framework requires a system of evaluation and classification that embraces wide areas of general environmental sensitivity as well as the particularly critical or *vital areas*. Such a system is especially needed where moving water is involved because one cannot simply protect an isolated *vital area* within an ecosystem, such as a grass bed or a coral reef, without regard for the condition of the surrounding waters.

87

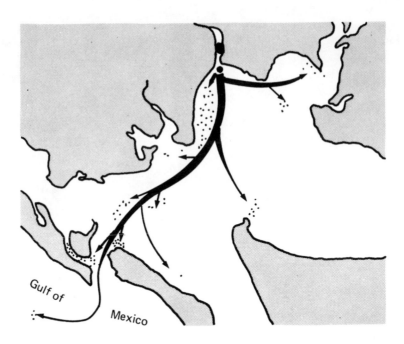

Figure 48. Outward migration of tagged brown shrimp from Galveston Bay (Englis, 1960).[56]

Such elements as these have been extensively degraded or destroyed by disturbances originating in the water some distance away; for example, by sediment loading of the water from dredging or by siltation of drainage courses in the shorelands by land clearing. Also, coastal aquatic species roam about for feeding or spawning and their young often are carried widely by the currents before settling down (clams, oysters, crabs, fish). Therefore, the *vital area* should be encompassed within a broader area of concern.

Areas of Environmental Concern

The "areas of concern" concept has developed concurrently in various Federal and state land planning studies over the past several years. Although it has been articulated in a variety of ways and has come to have a variety of implications, the basic concept remains the same—there are certain areas which, because of their attributes, require special management attention. Most often these attributes are environmental (natural), although sometimes they may include cultural (related to activities of mankind) values. As the concept is used here, it is limited to environmental considerations and the designation is: *area of environmental concern*. Such areas are identified as those where uncontrolled development might lead to significant adverse environmental impacts. Therefore, some restriction on use and some control on activity is required.

Four examples of various applications of this concept are given below:

1. Florida Environmental Land and Water Management Act of 1972:[57] "Areas of critical state concern" include those containing, or having a significant impact upon, environmental, historical, natural, or archaeological resources of regional or statewide importance, or those significantly affected by a major public facility or proposed area of major development potential.

2. California Coastal Zone Conservation Act of 1972:[58] "Areas of special biological significance" are identified for protection without concern for economic values because they contain biological communities of such extraordinary, even though unquantifiable, value that no acceptable risk of change in their environments as a result of man's activities can be entertained.

3. U.S. Senate Hearings on Coastal Zone Management Act:[59] "Areas of critical environmental concern" include areas where uncontrolled development could (1) result in irreversible damage to important historic values, cultural values, aesthetic values, natural systems or processes . . . or (2) unreasonably endanger life and property as a result of natural hazards of more than local significance. Coastal area examples are:

   a. coastal wetlands, marshes and other lands inundated by the tides;

   b. beaches and dunes;

   c. estuaries, shorelands, and floodplains of rivers, lakes and streams;

   d. rare or valuable ecosystems.

4. North Carolina Coastal Zone Management Act of 1973:[60] "Areas of particular public concern" may include the following:

   a. marshlands and estuarine waters;

   b. areas with significant impact upon environmental, historical or natural resources of regional or statewide importance;

   c. areas containing unique or fragile ecosystems which are not capable of withstanding uncontrolled development;

d. areas such as waterways and lands under or flowed by tidal waters or navigable waters, to which the state may be authorized to preserve, conserve or protect;

e. areas such as floodplains, beaches and dunelands wherein uncontrolled alteration or development increase the likelihood of flood damage and erosion and may necessitate large expenditures of public funds;

f. areas significantly affected by, or having a significant effect upon existing or proposed major public facilities or other areas of major public investment.

In summary, it appears that there is persuasive opinion that estuaries and their surrounding tidelands are *areas of environmental concern*. Furthermore, the importance of coastal flood plains to the coastal ecosystem indicates that they too should be designated as areas of environmental concern.

Areas of concern are a planning classification within which human activities must be controlled, though *not necessarily prohibited,* to protect the environment. Smaller areas for complete preservation—*vital areas*—are to be designated *within* areas of concern. As it works out, nearly all coastal flood plains and enclosed coastal waters, along with some nearshore coastal waters and coastal floodplains, are areas of environmental concern and therefore require special programs of environmental management on their behalf to ensure that a high level of ecosystem vitality is maintained.

Protection, Conservation, and Utilization

A concept of designation of land by three broad use categories has arisen out of attempts to plan for protection of ecologically sensitive areas. While the concept remains the same, various terms are used for the three categories. As used here they are termed *preservation, conservation* and *utilization* and the general proposition is termed the *PCU concept.* As an example, we discuss below the application of the PCU concept as it has been developed in Florida.

The Florida Coastal Coordinating Council has defined the following use designations for statewide coastal land classification:[61] "Preservation," no development suitable; "Conservation," carefully controlled development suitable; "Development," intensive development suitable. The factors utilized in selecting areas for these designations are:

a. Ecological significance of the area and its tolerance to alteration.

b. Water classification of adjacent water bodies.

c. Soil suitability of the area.

d. Susceptibility of the area to flooding, both from storm surge and runoff.

e. Archaeological and historical significance of the area.

f. Unique environmental features that may warrant protection.

The system has been adapted for the Collier County (Florida) Water Management District No. 6 study whereby land is classified for "preservation, conservation, or development" according to the following categories (see also Table 4):[62]

a. Preservation areas are those which provide invaluable public benefits—such as recreation, aesthetics, economic, and hurricane flood protection—and which are intolerant of development. These are areas which it is recommended should be preserved without any development and protected from degradation. "Preservation" areas include the waterways, mangroves, and marshes, which all form critical parts of the same productive and valuable coastal wetlands community.

b. Development areas are those areas which because of physiography, drainage, or other factors are comparatively suitable for development, and which have a reduced ecological, recreational, and public importance. Lands which could be developed directly or with only minor alteration would be classified as "development."

c. Conservation areas include the remaining lands, those marginally suitable for development and of important but non-critical ecological significance. These serve as a buffer between the preserved and the developed areas. They require special precautions when being developed. Because of flood and drainage problems, development in areas classified "conservation" is generally very expensive, both in terms of initial cost as well as continuing maintenance costs. Developments in these areas are potential hazards to both life and property and require the continual expenditure of public and private dollars to alleviate, prevent, or repair flood damage.

Comparison of Concepts

The PCU concept, as illustrated in the examples above, is perfectly compatible with the areas of concern concept. The *preservation* and *conservation* areas together are equivalent to *areas of environmental*

PRESERVATION	CONSERVATION	DEVELOPMENT
No construction, development or land alteration	Limited development— homes on fill islands (upland clusters) or stilts. Maximum density 1 du/ 5 acre	Intense development
No roads	Roads parallel to water flow or raised (trestle)	Adequately culverted roads
No canals or dredging— maintain historic (natural) overland water flow	No canals or dredging— cypress slough used to receive, cleanse and disperse water	No canals longer than 800 yards—drainage into man-made retention ponds, eventually to sloughs
Low intensity recreation (hunting, fishing, individual camping)	Moderate intensity recreation, with realization that areas may be periodically flooded	Intense recreation
No waste disposal	No solid waste disposal, dumps or landfills. Sewage by approved system	No dumps. Approval of DPC for sewage and solid waste disposal
No water consumption	Water consumption not to exceed 150 gpd/acre	Water consumption not to exceed 1,800 gpd/acre
No removal of vegetation	Maximum 5% vegetation removed, except for exotics. Only native vegetation used for landscaping	Maximum 40% vegetation removed, except exotics. No melalogua or Brazilian pepper used

Table 4. Land Use Constraints recommended for Collier County, Florida.[62]

concern. Also, the *preservation area* concept coincides with the *vital area* concept. The parallelism of these systems is shown in the following comparisons:

> *Vital Areas* or Preservation Areas: Ecosystem elements of such critical importance and high value that they are to be preserved intact and protected from harmful outside forces; normally encompassed *within* an area of environmental concern.

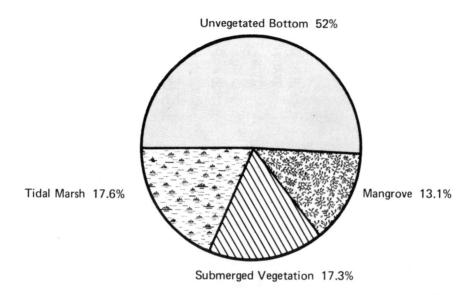

Figure 49. The percentage of mangrove swamp, tidal marsh, submerged vegetation, and unvegetated bottom in estuaries of the west coast of Florida.[63]

> *Areas of Environmental Concern* or Conservation Areas: Broad areas of environmental sensitivity (often containing one or more *vital areas*), the development or use of which must be carefully controlled to protect the ecosystem.
> *Areas of General Use* or Utilization Areas: Areas where only the normal levels of caution are required in utilization and in development activity.

Effect of Use Restriction

Vital areas may take up a moderate part of the immediate coastal waters province in low-lying areas with rich aquatic ecosystems characterized by much vegetation, shellfish beds, and so forth. For example, the estuarine water areas of the west coast of Florida are, on the average, about 50 percent vegetated *vital areas* (mangrove, marsh, submerged grasses), as shown in Figure 49.[63] Wetlands and vegetated tideflats (*vital areas*) make up about 2.3 percent of the area of all coastal counties.[3]

The areas of environmental concern make up a larger but not unreasonable fraction of available surface. For example, estuaries in their

State	Hard and Soft Clams [1] (Acres)	Oysters [1] (Acres)	Bay Scallops [1] (Acres)	Wetlands [2] (Acres)	Tidelands [3] (Acres)	Estuaries [4] (Acres)	Territorial Sea Area [5] (Acres)	State land Area [6] (Acres)
Me.	355,000	200	—	16,178	1,455	39,400	437,760	21,257,600
N.H.	5,000	2,000	—	5,285	375	12,400	24,960	5,954,560
Mass.	28,000	1,500	10,000	34,520	7,940	207,000	368,640	5,284,480
R.I.	22,000	1,000	4,000	1,360	645	94,700	76,800	776,960
Ct.	20,000	40,000	2,000	6,909	2,077	31,600	—	3,205,760
N.Y.	315,000	10,000	40,000	24,855	11,530	376,600	243,840	31,728,640
N.J.	300,000	60,000	1,000	150,440	20,870	778,400	249,600	5,015,040
Del.	15,000	20,000	—	49,578	43,756	395,500	53,760	1,316,480
Md.	250,000	326,000	—	117,840	15,890	1,406,100	59,920	6,769,280
Va.	300,000	384,000	—	44,950	86,100	1,670,000	215,040	26,122,880
N.C.	100,000	200,000	40,000	100,450	58,400	2,206,000	577,920	33,655,040
S.C.	2,000	20,000	—	91,000	345,000	427,900	359,040	19,875,200
Ga.	—	15,000	—	75,500	285,650	170,800	192,000	37,680,640
Fla.	1,000	15,000	—	134,600	158,200	1,051,200	1,113,600	37,478,400
Total	1,713,000	1,094,700	97,000	853,465	1,037,888	8,868,200	3,972,480	236,120,960

[1] Acreage of "important shellfish habitat," per reference 64.
[2] From page 4, reference 64.
[3] From page 4, reference 64.
[4] From page 30, reference 3.
[5] Coastline miles x 3, reference 65.
[6] Reference 65.

Table 5. Amount of certain vital areas in the Atlantic Coastal Zone.

entirety are estimated to make up less than 10 percent of all the area (land and water) of the U.S. coastal counties.

In Table 5 we have tabulated available statistics for the Atlantic Coast states (not available for Gulf or Pacific) on the area of land, water, and of *vital areas* for comparison. Here it can be seen that wetlands and vegetated tidelands together make up only about one percent of all state land and water areas. Of coastal waters alone, they make up 15 percent, of which about half, the tidelands, are presumed to be in the public domain. The public domain extends up to the mean high water (MHW) line in the Atlantic States (except Virginia, where it extends to low water). The seven percent above MHW—the wetlands—are the only areas where a private landower might be denied use by a management program.

Other *vital areas* that need protection take up even less of total state areas; for example, oyster beds comprise about 0.5 percent of total lands and coastal waters and about 8 percent of the coastal waters province.

The Coastal Floodplain

Because of its particular ecologic character, the coastal floodplain is to be designated an *area of environmental concern* (or conservation area) to be left undeveloped or to be protected by stringent controls, such as we have suggested in our discussions of shorelands (page 37). The coastal floodplain belt follows the shoreline and encompasses many of the estuarine *vital areas*. Thus the floodplain can serve as a buffer area to protect *vital areas* that lie along the shoreline—such as vegetated tidelands and tidal flats. The floodplain buffer protects the wetlands and tidelands from runoff surge and heavier loads of sediment and other pollutants than they can take up (page 71).

Where development is to be allowed in the floodplain there should be somewhat more stringent controls than in the shorelands above them in order to prevent: (1) erosion and general urban pollution, (2) diversion or disruption of natural drainage patterns and (3) loss of critical habitat for coastal species. This will usually require a low density of occupancy and constraints on landscaping, on waste disposal, on application of fertilizer and pesticides and so forth.[66] These constraints are particularly important where the floodplain drains into a small embayment or lagoon with a restricted rate of flushing (page 44). There are also natural hazards to habitation in coastal floodplains as explained in the next section.

In designating the floodplain area, it will be convenient to use the 100-year storm recurrence value, or "100-year floodplain" because many

95

Federal and state floodplain management criteria are based upon this water level (page 99). However, for specific local reasons, it may be more appropriate to designate the "25-year" or other statistical floodplain, depending upon land slope, drainage characteristics, soil type or other variables.

Natural Hazards

There are special risks attached to development in any shorelands within reach of coastal storm or flood tides. On the open coast, the risks are mostly involved with the direct onslaught of storm-driven waves (Figure 50). In the estuaries, risks are involved with storm-induced high waters.

The ocean coast is in a dynamic equilibrium between two factors: (1) the erosive forces of storm winds and waves and (2) the restorative powers of prevailing geologic, oceanic, and meteorological actions (Figure 51). In response to the interplay of these forces, the whole system of beaches, barrier islands and dunes shifts more or less continuously.

Clearly, this is a risky place to maintain habitation. The costs in loss of property and life have been high for many beachfronts. Furthermore, the enormous private and public investments to stabilize and safeguard these inhabited beaches with structures have not often been rewarded with success. High energy natural processes undermine the bulkheads, erode sand from behind the groins, and throw damaging breakers over the bulwarks.

A related function of dunes is to serve as a storage area for sand to replace that eroded by waves or torn away by storms and thus to provide long-term stability to the shorefront (page 33). Because dune formations are fragile, activities of man that cause even slight alterations to them may lead to significant disruptions. Once the barrier dune is weakened, its valuable functions are impaired and it no longer serves its unique protective role.

Although estuarine areas do not receive the wave pounding that ocean beaches do, they often suffer persistent erosion, particularly those characterized by a soil-bank front. Eroding shores must be bulkheaded or else the buildings must be set back a considerable distance from the bank edge. A setback allows the area between the bank and the building to be left as a naturally vegetated *buffer area* for cleansing of runoff waters and for scenic purposes. Where bulkheads are required and feasible they should be built behind the tideland or wetland vegetation (Figure 52).

But even on estuarine shores there are risks from storm flooding and therefore building must be closely regulated. The shorelines of enclosed

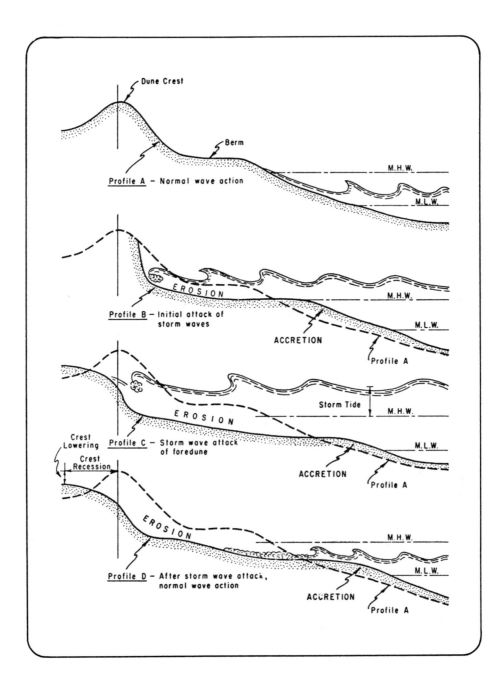

Figure 50. Schematic diagram of storm wave attack on beach and dune.[67]

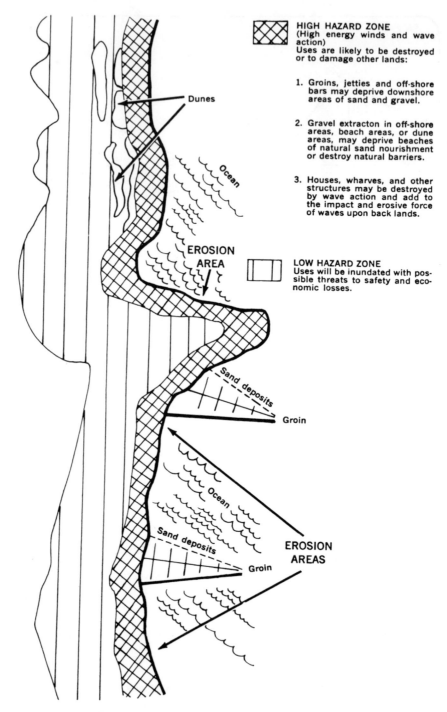

HIGH HAZARD ZONE
(High energy winds and wave action)
Uses are likely to be destroyed or to damage other lands:

1. Groins, jetties and off-shore bars may deprive downshore areas of sand and gravel.

2. Gravel extracton in off-shore areas, beach areas, or dune areas, may deprive beaches of natural sand nourishment or destroy natural barriers.

3. Houses, wharves, and other structures may be destroyed by wave action and add to the impact and erosive force of waves upon back lands.

LOW HAZARD ZONE
Uses will be inundated with possible threats to safety and economic losses.

Dunes

Ocean

EROSION AREA

Sand deposits

Groin

Ocean

Sand deposits

Groin

EROSION AREAS

Figure 51. Coastal flood hazard zones.[25]

Figure 52. Bulkheads are to be placed behind the grass line of vegetated shorelines (Thomas Barnard, Virginia Institute of Marine Science).

water bodies are protected from the direct force of storm waves, but subject to damage from high waters caused by winter storms or hurricanes. Storm flooding may reach 12 feet or more above normal tide level in certain areas, inundating large areas of habitation and causing extensive property damage and risk to human life. U.S. Department of Housing and Urban Development regulations permit Federal insurance protection for structures in flood hazard areas only if floodproofed or built on pilings with the main floor above the 100-year flood level.[68] Some coastal areas are now requiring all development to meet the Federal requirements.

In addition, land fill, clearing of vegetative cover, surfacing and other development in the floodplain reduce the absorptive capacity of the land for storm water. The enhanced runoff surge adds to the level of flood waters in confined estuaries and heightens storm damage. An example of the effect of urbanization on stream discharge peaks is shown in Figure 53.

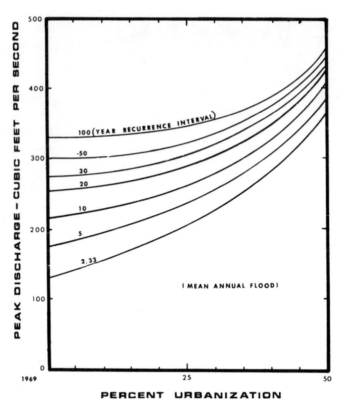

Figure 53. The effect of urbanization on peak stream discharge (Mercer Creek, Washington).[6]

Stringent control of building is required in coastal flood plains subject to hurricane inundation, as shown in the following summary from a U.S. Army Corps of Engineers report on the problem in Florida:[69]

1. The only buildings on filled land which are safe from destruction by tides are those on fill 20 feet above sea level.

2. Buildings at ground level on concrete slabs or other foundations, even though otherwise well constructed, are easily demolished by a tidal surge.

3. Coastal roads, streets and expressways at low elevations are subject to flooding and often become impassable several hours, or even days, prior to the onslaught of a hurricane. Also, bridges, causeways and access roads are often put out of commission in advance of, or in the early stages of a hurricane, thus rendering them useless for evacuation.

4. Seawalls and bulkheads are no protection against hurricane tides and often increase beach erosion with resultant collapse of shoreside buildings.

Alteration of Coastal Water Basins *

Any excavation or construction in a coastal water basin bears the burden of "presumption of adverse ecologic effects." Changes of shape of basins, release of sediments, elimination of *vital areas,* blockage of circulation or installation of structures all have a potential for damage to coastal ecosystems. Dredging activity is the greatest single threat to coastal waters.

Dredging, the excavation of bottom material, and *filling,* the deposition of materials into the bottom, are construction techniques used widely in the coastal zone. Dredging may be performed to create and maintain canals, navigation channels, turning basins, harbors and marinas, for laying pipeline and as a source of material for fill or construction. Filling relates to the deposition of dredged materials, either for the specific purpose of creating new dry or fast land, for commercial, industrial, residential or other uses, or as disposal of the by-product (dredge spoil) produced during dredging.

By 1967, the U.S. Department of the Interior reported that the nation had lost 7.1 percent of its important fish and wildlife estuarine habitat.[105] This loss varies significantly with locale, with California having destroyed 67 percent of its estuaries, New York 16 percent and New Jersey 13 percent. More recently, it was estimated that 23 percent of the United States' estuaries have been severely modified, and 50 percent moderately so.[106]

An example of the amount of such area eliminated in one state is shown below for the Texas coastal zone (data to 1966):[109]

	Channel Area (Acres)	Spoil Area (Acres)	Total Area (Acres)
Open estuary	7,590	30,320	37,910
Tide flats	920	3,920	4,840
Vegetated tidelands	6,980	23,000	29,980
	15,490	57,240	72,730

Dredge and fill activities adversely affect the coastal ecosystem in a variety of ways. They can create short and long-term changes in water currents, circulation, mixing, flushing and salinity; add to the water turbidity, siltation and pollution; and lower the dissolved oxygen.

---

* This section was adapted from a paper by Dr. Edward T. LaRoe, Office of Coastal Environment, National Oceanic and Atmospheric Administration, U.S. Department of Commerce, Washington, D. C.

101

The most obvious effect of dredge and fill is the direct destruction of habitat. Submerged bottoms or coastal wetlands and tidelands, along with their associated organisms, are directly destroyed by these processes. Dredging also produces spoil which must be disposed of, and filling requires some area to be dredged for a source of fill material; such operations cause a two-fold destruction of habitat that extends beyond the area of primary concern.

In addition to the direct loss of habitat which accompanies dredge-and-fill, the removal, transportation and deposition of sediment creates and disperses large quantities of silt and debris into coastal waters (page 148). The finer particles can be carried for extensive distances—over one-half-mile—before settling out.[107] Suspended silt in high concentrations creates a number of adverse environmental impacts (page 21).

Coarse sediments which promote interstitial water circulation also aid aeration of the subsurface layers. This aerobic state is necessary for the development of a healthy, productive bottom community. Fine sediments created by dredging can seal the bottom, reducing interstitial circulation.

By increasing turbidity, suspended silt decreases light penetration into the water, reducing photosynthesis.

Estuarine sediments also act as a pollutant trap or sink. Many kinds of pollutants, including heavy metals and pesticides, are adsorbed onto the sediments. Dredging operations resuspend these in the water column, increasing the hazardous exposure to plants and animals. The silt suspension may also increase nutrient release, leading to eutrophic blooms.

The conditions which result from dredge and fill activities create other long-term problems beyond the immediate and direct impact. Destruction of the vegetated bottoms and replacement with loose sediments—dredged bottoms, cut channels with barren banks and spoil or fill deposits, for example—induces future erosion creating an extended problem of high turbidities.

As silt deposits from dredging accumulate in the estuary, they form a "false bottom." Characterized by shifting, unstable sediments, the dredged bottoms, fill deposits, and spoil areas are only slowly, if at all, repopulated. The larvae of bottom dwelling animals such as oysters, snails and crustaceans will not settle on soft sediments.

Bottoms deepened by dredging below the depth of light penetration are not populated by grasses or algae.[108] Depressions (either basins or channels), as well as fill areas or spoil banks, can result in changed water circulation, eventually causing changes in water temperature, salinity, dissolved oxygen, sediment accumulation and ultimately productivity.

If one portion of an estuary is isolated from another by long spoil banks, large portions of estuarine areas can be degraded or removed as a productive unit from the total system.

The stagnant waters in artificially deepened areas or man-made basins have reduced oxygen and act as sediment traps. These sediments lower water quality and productivity in three ways: the area itself is unproductive; low quality water slowly leaches out affecting neighboring waters; and during storms large volumes of accumulated debris and anaerobic sediments may be flushed out causing a sudden reduction of water quality and stress to surrounding organisms.

Vegetation

Hydrologic factors control the abundance and diversity of plantlife in coastal areas and therefore determine the natural patterns of vegetation. Topography, water quality and soil condition are closely associated factors. Many aspects of coastal land use management relate to the patterns of vegetation. On the one hand, certain *vital areas* are to be preserved because of the ecologic value of their vegetation. On the other hand, patterns of vegetation are the key to identification of land and water capability types and therefore a basis of land use evaluation and classification.

An inventory of vegetation required for planning purposes can be accomplished by following the natural zonation of vegetation, as controlled by the joint influences of fresh and salt water: the tides are particularly important, as shown in Figure 54. Various designations of tidal and storm water levels are explained in Figure 55. The following is a convenient classification of natural vegetation (keyed in Figure 54):

Shorelands
1. Upland vegetation
2. Floodplain vegetation

Coastal Waters Province
3. Wetland vegetation
4. Tideland vegetation
5. Submerged vegetation
6. Barrier island vegetation

Wetlands and tidelands are elements of the coastal waters province, being covered by tidewater permanently or at certain stages of the normal yearly tidal and storm cycle. Floodplain vegetation and vegetation of the coastal watershed are elements of the shorelands.

Each of the above six classes may be further divided into categories representing recognizable vegetation subzones. For example, wetlands

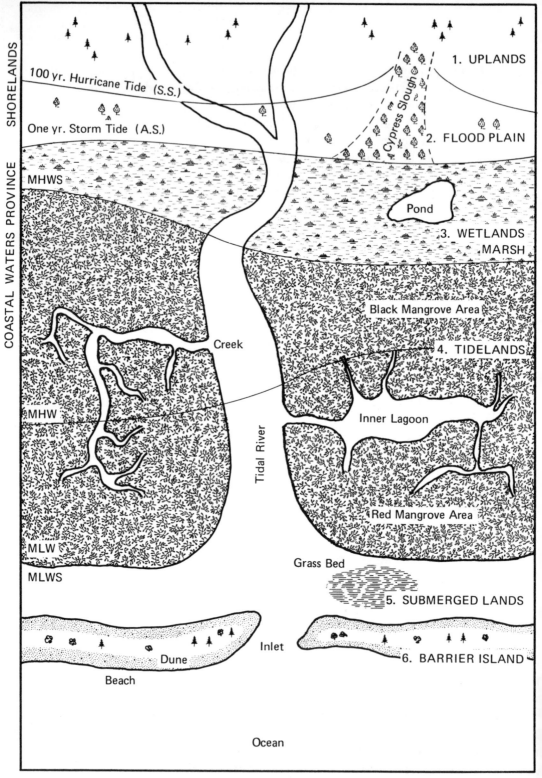

Figure 54. Vegetative zonation of a hypothetical mangrove coastal area in Southwest Florida. See text for details (not to scale).

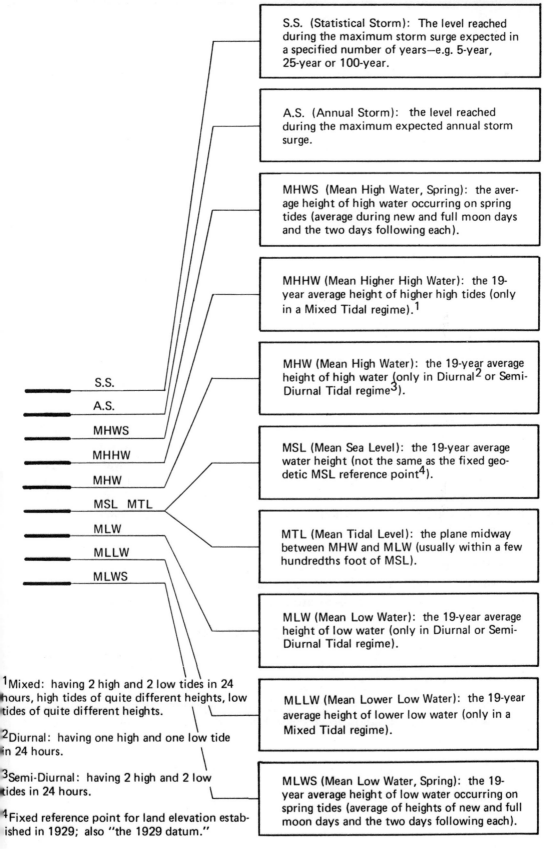

S.S. (Statistical Storm): The level reached during the maximum storm surge expected in a specified number of years—e.g. 5-year, 25-year or 100-year.

A.S. (Annual Storm): the level reached during the maximum expected annual storm surge.

MHWS (Mean High Water, Spring): the average height of high water occurring on spring tides (average during new and full moon days and the two days following each).

MHHW (Mean Higher High Water): the 19-year average height of higher high tides (only in a Mixed Tidal regime).[1]

MHW (Mean High Water): the 19-year average height of high water (only in Diurnal[2] or Semi-Diurnal Tidal regime[3]).

MSL (Mean Sea Level): the 19-year average water height (not the same as the fixed geodetic MSL reference point[4]).

MTL (Mean Tidal Level): the plane midway between MHW and MLW (usually within a few hundredths foot of MSL).

MLW (Mean Low Water): the 19-year average height of low water (only in Diurnal or Semi-Diurnal Tidal regime).

MLLW (Mean Lower Low Water): the 19-year average height of lower low water (only in a Mixed Tidal regime).

MLWS (Mean Low Water, Spring): the 19-year average height of low water occurring on spring tides (average of heights of new and full moon days and the two days following each).

S.S.
A.S.
MHWS
MHHW
MHW
MSL MTL
MLW
MLLW
MLWS

[1]Mixed: having 2 high and 2 low tides in 24 hours, high tides of quite different heights, low tides of quite different heights.

[2]Diurnal: having one high and one low tide in 24 hours.

[3]Semi-Diurnal: having 2 high and 2 low tides in 24 hours.

[4]Fixed reference point for land elevation established in 1929; also "the 1929 datum."

Figure 55. Reference heights for coastal waters.

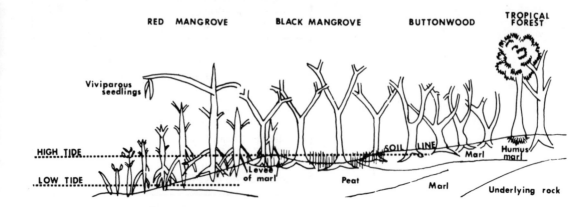

RED MANGROVE   BLACK MANGROVE   BUTTONWOOD   TROPICAL FOREST

Figure 56. Diagrammatic cross-section of a mangrove swamp (after Davis, 1940; Kurz and Wagner, 1957).[63]

may contain separate red and black mangrove subzones (Figure 56).

For the most general planning purposes one may identify the vegetation zones as they progress down the land-water gradient. But to meet legal requirements for restrictive management programs, a professional botanist or ecologist usually will have to identify the species of plants and locate the boundaries between vegetative zones with precision.

Vegetation will also be the key to the location of shoreland drainageways, *vital areas*, which are to be preserved to protect the rate of flow and the purity of runoff waters that discharge to coastal water basins. For example, in Florida, cypress trees are a reliable indicator of wet ground drainage areas (Figure 57). In each area there will be plant species known to professional ecologists that indicate drainageways.

The sea grasses occur over submerged bottoms in patterns of succession that are related to depth and other variables—salinity, temperature, turbidity, currents and so forth. At present, there is no basis to discriminate between the ecological value of different seagrasses, or their life requirements. All grassbeds are to be preserved as *vital areas*.

USE ALLOCATION

The system of evaluation of land and water resource capabilities that we have outlined lends itself to various methods of use allocation and to physical planning. To demonstrate, we have mapped out a number of the categories as they might apply to a hypothetical area of coastal waters and shorelands in a coastal ecosystem of high environmental sensitivity.

106

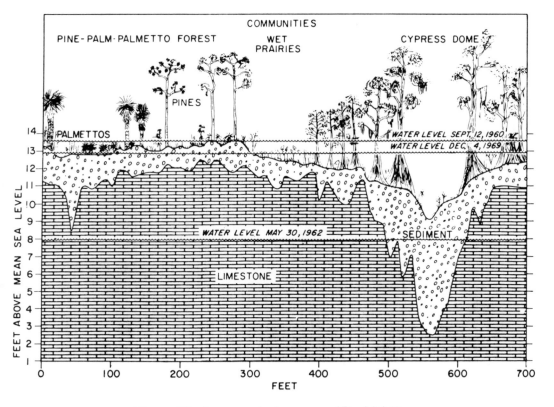

Figure 57. Cypress drainageway (Florida).[70]

Water

We have seen that coastal land and water use management has to recognize the principle: *Water provides the essential connection of land and sea elements of the coastal ecosystem* (page   4). Thus water management in its many aspects is a primary consideration—beginning with the coastal watershed.

The methodology for identifying watersheds and drawing watershed divides in a shoreland area is essentially the same as for any area. For effective environmental planning it is desirable to delineate the smallest identifiable drainage basins as watersheds. Some of the flow may drain to channels, some to intermittent drainageways, and some directly to estuarine or ocean waters. In Figure 58 we have indicated drainage basin divides and the resulting watershed areas. These are areas that directly affect coastal waters through runoff.

Floodplain boundaries are set by various methods, none of which are too reliable for long "storm return intervals," say 50 or 100 years, because

107

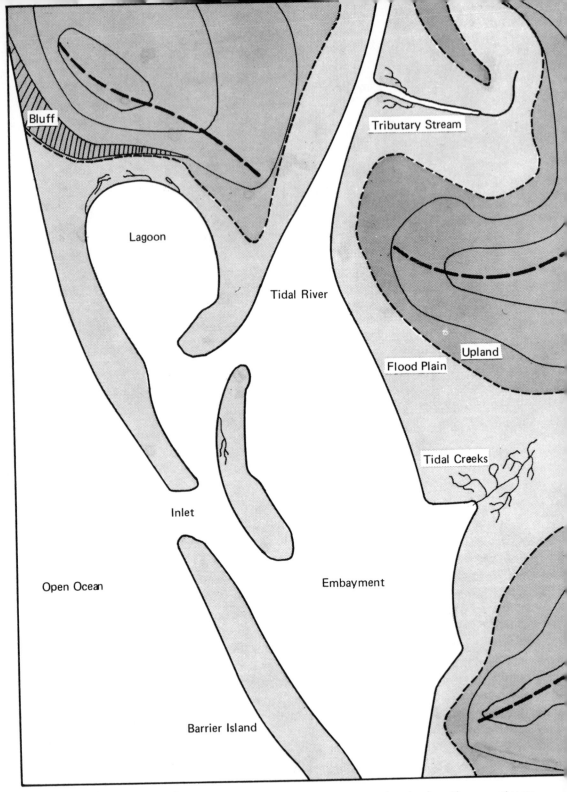

Figure 58. Example coastal area, water map: land elevation contours (solid lines); watershed divides (heavy dashed lines); flood plain maximum water level boundary (light dashed line); water basin types.

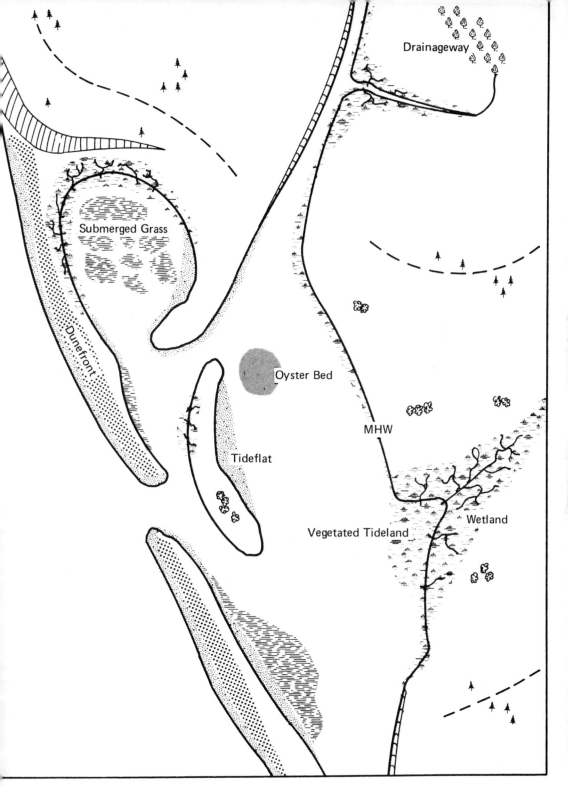

Figure 59. Example coastal area, *vital areas.*

accurate historical records are not usually available. Nevertheless, this must be accomplished for a number of purposes in most coastal communities and the information should become available for coastal planning purposes. Vegetation may be a poor indicator of long interval storms.

The floodplain is the part of the shorelands that has some probability of being inundated during storms. At those times it has a direct connection with coastal waters. We have drawn in the upper boundary of the floodplain in Figure 58. The lower limit would be the yearly storm height, as indicated by the upper boundary of the wetlands.

The coastal water basin should be investigated as to its circulation type, depth, form and geology so that water and land use can be managed in respect to such limitations. The special vulnerabilities of water basins guide policies for water traffic, waste disposal, navigation channel dredging, shoreland development and so forth. Normally, the most fundamental criterion will be the degree of water exchange or flushing rate of the water basin. The basin types involved in the hypothetical ecosystem are shown in Figure 58.

Vegetation and Protection Areas

Vegetation is the identifying characteristic of many *vital areas:* drainageways in the shorelands and wetlands, vegetated tidelands, and submerged grass beds in the coastal waters province. These *vital areas* are designated in Figure 59. In a management program one would conduct a rather exhaustive survey of vegetation in drainageway corridors and in the floodplains, wetlands, tidelands and bottoms. A somewhat less detailed survey would be appropriate for general shorelands.

Fixed *vital areas,* both above and below the tidelands, are quite amenable to mapping, but transient ones provide difficulties. Transient *vital areas* are most often water masses of special ecological value which shift position with wind, tide, runoff inflow and so forth. In any event, to obtain boundaries of sufficient accuracy to serve regulatory needs, a professional ecologist must be engaged. Examples of fixed vital areas are shown in Figure 59.

110

CHAPTER 4

Constraints on Specific Uses

In planning for coastal land- and water-use management, it is necessary to identify, through impact assessment, the ecosystem hazards associated with specific types of utilization. Some types of use involve construction of projects which would lead to gross disturbance of the ecosystem. Other uses might endanger or preempt space from ecologically *vital areas.* Still others might cause day-after-day occupancy or operating disturbances lasting for the duration of their existence (Table 6).

Environmental constraints on specific uses involve the following aspects: (1) location of the use, (2) design and placement of structures, (3) control of construction activities, and (4) control of operational or occupancy modes. The first two are planning functions; the second two require attention in planning but are mostly involved with enforcement of performance standards.

In this chapter we provide information on the adverse effects to be expected from particular types of uses. Each use description discusses specific effects and feasible control methods in relation to location, design and performance requirements during construction and operation.

The suggested constraints are designed toward a single goal: the achievement of *best ecosystem function.* This goal parallels our general theme; namely, that with effective planning and management, coastal ecosystems can be maintained at high levels of health even while urbanization of the coastal zone increases. This will require foregoing many economic ventures and community programs. But we believe the trade-offs can be accomplished without serious penalty through innovative management programs. Consequently, the constraints we recommend are written from one basic presumption: *It is a desirable and achievable national goal to maintain coastal ecosystems at their highest and best ecologic condition. To accomplish this, adverse ecologic disturbances must be reduced to a minimum.*

AIRPORTS

Urban airports often have been located at the water's edge, where large tracts of wetlands and tidelands are available at low prices and

111

Economic and Population Growth	Some Major Resulting Agents of Modification		Identified Stressed Systems Related to These Activities	The Multiple-Stressed System: Ecology of The Future?	Some Components in the Resulting Multiple-Stressed System
1. Urban-Suburban Expansion in Response to Population Growth and Economic Opportunity		Municipal	Sewage Wastes Seafood Wastes	Example of One Major Economic Component →	Development of Petrochemical Complexes
	1. Waste Discharge	Industrial	Pesticides	Resulting Activities	
2. General Economic Growth Diversification, and Sophistication		Agricultural	Thermal Wastes Radioactive Wastes Papermill Wastes	Waste Discharge	Sewage Waste
3. Expansion of Specific Activities Related to the Estuarine Zone		Navigation		--Municipal --Industrial	Dredging Spoil
	2. Dredging	Mining and Processing	Dredging Spoil Phosphate Waste Destruction of Wetlands	--Ships	Impoundments
--Marine Fisheries				Transportation	Petroleum Stores
		Land Development	Altered Currents Salinities, etc.	Dredging and Filling	Pilings
--Civilian and National Defense Transporation					Brine Pollution
--Marine Mining and Processing		Fresh Water Impoundment Diversion, etc.		Population Growth and in-migration	Petrochemicals
--Outdoor Recreation	3. Physical Structures	Piers, jetties, Hurricane Barriers, etc.	Impoundments Acid Waters Brine Pollution	Development of Secondary and Marginal Activities	Etc.
--Waste Discharge				Shoreline Development, etc.	
		Aids to Navigation			

Table 6. Selected elements of estuarine ecological change due to man's influence.[3]

where an unobstructed overwater approach path is available. Consequently, much *vital area* has been preempted. As a rule, terminal, parking lot and runway configurations are to be chosen to minimize encroachment on *vital areas* such as wetlands, tidelands and drainageways.

Location is the most critical airport planning considerations for environmental reasons. For example, airport construction in the coastal floodplain above the wetlands can cause significant damage to the coastal ecosystem through elimination of wildlife habitats, interruption of surface and groundwater flow and serious degradation of water quality. Therefore, new airports are to be located upland of the coastal floodplain in order to minimize impact on wetlands and coastal waters.

Both construction activities and the operation of airports cause ecologic disturbances, but providing that reasonable construction performance standards are enforced on contractors, the chronic problems of operations will be the more serious.

The extensive surfaced areas of airports increase the runoff of surface water contaminated by oil, biocides and jet exhaust particulates. These pollutants seriously disturb the ecosystems of surrounding coastal waters. Therefore, it is necessary that all runoff water be collected and restored by treatment before discharge to any coastal water basin.

Airports are to be separated from vital areas by a buffer strip of vegetated land; this would normally include all the coastal floodplain area. The buffer serves to filter and purify the runoff from the airport

112

after it has been collected by storm drains and treated. Pre-treated runoff is released into the buffer area for final polishing before it reaches coastal waters (see page 40).

Aircraft bird strikes, noise, and emissions are damaging to surrounding natural communities. A solution is to select takeoff and land approach patterns that produce the least damage to these communities. Recommended Constraints:

1. Coastal ecosystems are to be protected from airports by buffer strips.

2. Airports are to be located above coastal floodplains, using them as a buffer.

3. Runways and facilities are to be designed to minimize paved surfaces.

4. Runoff from the airport complex is to be collected and restored before discharge (perhaps into buffer strip vegetation).

RESIDENTIAL LAND CARE

The everyday use of biocides and fertilizers is an inconspicuous but prevalent threat to coastal ecosystems. The widespread use of these chemicals by individual homeowners may add up to a major disturbance where there is a proliferation of shoreline homesites.

Water runoff transports biocides and fertilizers to coastal waters either by natural runoff or by community drainage systems. Biocides may be directly toxic or they may enter food chains and gradually build up to critical levels in many species. Fertilizers cause nutrient enrichment of the water, which leads to overfertilization and oxygen reduction from pollution by nutrients, principally nitrates (page 19).

The degree of damage is related to: proximity of the application area to the water, type of vegetation in the flow course, time and method of application, the slope of the land, the type of soil, the type of drainage and the amount of runoff.

In order to protect coastal waters, traditional practices in the use of biocides and fertilizers must be changed. Application of these chemicals can be avoided or much reduced by voluntary homeowner action, by regulating the use or sale of products, and by substitution of improved products.

Storm drain systems, incorporating controlled grading of development sites to direct runoff, offer a possible solution through collection and treatment of runoff water, providing that the effluent is cleansed properly and its discharge rate regulated (page 40). Recommended buffer areas between shoreland residential areas and coastal waters guarantee added protection from direct surface runoff into coastal water bodies.

Recommended Constraints:

    1. Biocide and fertilizer use on private lands in coastal watersheds is to be avoided where possible or reduced to the minimum.

    2. Application of biocides and fertilizers is to be controlled in respect to conditions of: soils, slopes, erosion patterns and water runoff, proximity of coastal water and vegetation in flow course.

    3. Buffer areas are to be provided between shoreland residences and coastal waters of a size to correlate with the extent of shoreline development.

    4. Water collected by storm drains is to be cleansed by treatment and its discharge regulated.

MARINAS AND PIERS

The growth of pleasure boating has accentuated construction of new marinas and related waterfront development. As environmental restrictions increase, the centralized marina becomes a solution to the greater problem of innumerable private docksites. Increases in size and range of services of the marina, however, present their own problems of environmental impact. The significant determinants of this impact include: the location of the marina, site preparation and construction, modifications required to make that site practicable and design of the facility.

Locating marinas as much as possible in places that provide natural protection and accessibility greatly minimizes environmental impact. Similarly, marinas must be designed for minimum interference with *vital areas* and adequate control of pollutants.

Marinas on estuaries with restricted flushing rates endanger aquatic biota because of the waterbody's inability to rid itself of marina-source contaminants. Extensive surfacing for parking lots and drives leads to rapid runoff of contaminated water unless controlled. Where there is an inadequate natural harbor, breakwaters required to protect the marina may interfere with tides and currents.

Vital areas such as vegetated tidelands and wetlands are to be avoided as sites for land fill and surfacing. *Essential* shoreline structures are to be placed so as to preempt a minimum of these areas. Marinas are to be located so as to minimize severe environmental impacts that result from required channel and basin dredging. Marinas should not be sited so as to require the excavation of man-made canals, particularly dead end canals which have restricted flushing capacity.

Where a marina site requires excavation for utilities, building foundations, fill or canals, the potential for erosion and sedimentation in nearby waters is increased. Increased stream flow from clearing and surfacing cause erosion, sedimentation, downstream flooding and the introduction of high nutrient loads into estuarine waters.

Ancillary marina facilities, such as parking areas, boat storage housing, and repair yards, are to be situated above the wetlands and insofar as possible out of the coastal floodplains so as to displace the effects of surfacing and clearing and the pollution potential to less sensitive areas. An internalized drainage system which would collect and restore water runoff and other liquid waste is to be installed. Sewage facilities are to be designed for maximum capacity. Construction on the waterfront, such as docks, piers, and walkways, should be elevated on pilings and not landfill.

Recommended Constraints:

1. Marinas are to be located in naturally protected harbors with steep shores where the least amount of alteration of *vital areas* is required.
2. Water basins with poor flushing are to be avoided as marina sites.
3. Supporting marina facilities, such as winter storage yards, are to be located inland.
4. Impervious surfacing on the waterfront is to be avoided to the maximum extent and effective storm drain systems are to be installed.
5. Pilings are to be used to elevate marina structures rather than solid fill.
6. Pump-out facilities for boat sewage must be provided.

AGRICULTURE

Ecologic disturbances resulting from agriculture in the coastal area of the United States include sedimentation, nutrient enrichment and toxicity—caused by soils, fertilizers, animal wastes and biocides carried into tidal waters with surface runoff and stream flow (Figure 60).[71] Also, disruption of the natural runoff pattern (quantity, quality and rate of flow), occurs by diking, drainage and irrigation works. Proximity to coastal waters (and to the feeder streams) is the major factor controlling the severity of the impacts.

Ecosystem disturbances from agriculture can be reduced by effective management of ongoing farm practices and by locating those types of agriculture with high pollution potential out of floodplain areas. Erosion

115

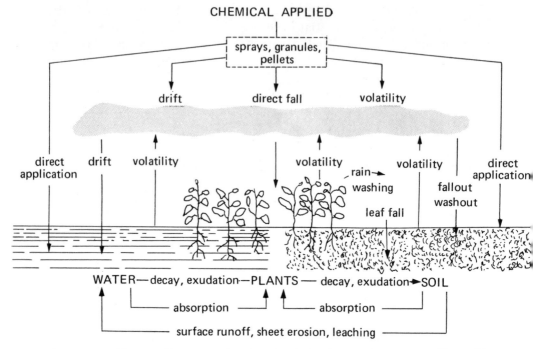

Figure 60. The cycling of toxic chemicals in the environment. (From Foy and Bingham.) [72]

and hydrologic problems can be adequately controlled through use of current standard principles of sound soil and water conservation.

Erosion is to be curbed so as to reduce discharge of soil into waterways as follows: by using improved methods of preparing land for cultivation, such as contouring, contour-stripcropping and terracing; by planting all idle sections; and by controlling the density of livestock in easily eroded pastures.

A ranking of national sediment yields from seven types of nonpoint sources shows that cropland yields four times more sediment to public waters than any other erosion-causing activity: [72]

	Total Sediment Yield Relative Ranking
Undisturbed Forest	1
Grassland	10
Abandoned Mines	20
Active Surface Mines	40
Disturbed Forests	40
Construction	50
Cropland	200

116

Cropland thus contributes about 45% of the total load of four billion tons of sediment generated per year in the United States, construction about 10% and the other sources smaller percentages.

Eutrophication (nutrient overenrichment of waters) is reduced by practices which: reduce the amount of fertilizer needed, increase the efficiency of its uptake by crops or improve its retention on croplands. It is particularly important to control nitrate fertilizers because nitrogen controls plant production in coastal waters and nitrate leeching and runoff can severely degrade adjacent coastal ecosystems through eutrophication (page 19).

Corrective practices for animal waste pollution include collection and treatment of the wastes, controlled utilization of them onsite as fertilizer and eliminating or severely reducing the runoff from waste accumulations.

More than 50 percent of U.S. sales of biocides go to farm use. Biocide pollution is to be mitigated by prohibiting the use of DDT, Aldrin, Dieldrin, and other "hard" pesticides in favor of relatively benign or short-lived compounds. Such controls will abate toxicity of coastal waters from cropland runoff into the coastal drainage.

Neither the pattern of water drainage nor the alignment of water courses are to be altered such that the timing and volume of flows is significantly upset. The goal is to retain the natural pattern of flow (page 10). Land drainage should be arranged so that cropland runoff slowly filters through sufficient buffer area of natural vegetation before reaching public waterways to remove contaminants and to prevent runoff surges (page 42).

To the maximum extent possible, farmlands should be located out of the floodplain and away from tidal creeks, wetlands and tidelands (*vital areas*). An effective means of retarding the impact of farm pollutants is to set all farms and feedlots back from the water edge by a buffer strip of natural vegetation. The strip is to be wide enough that the natural filtration ability of soil and vegetation can cleanse the runoff water of significant contamination. Coastal area planning should incorporate the buffer strip feature as part of the environmental control plan of agriculture. The buffer strip has other benefits than runoff purification; e.g., stabilization of erodible banks by leaving natural vegetation in place (Figure 61).

The success of some crops—salt hay, rice, artichokes—depends upon proximity to the coastal area for suitable soil, water and other conditions, and cultivation of these away from the coast may not be feasible. Also, agricultural land use preserves open space in coastal areas for its scenic and aesthetic values and if through proper management significant disturbances are eliminated, this use is most desirable. Another advantage

117

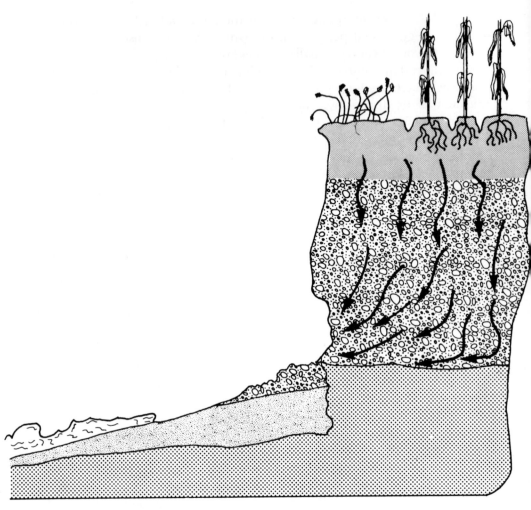

Figure 61. Cultivation increases soil permeability which accelerates bank erosion, Chesapeake Bay, Maryland. Buffer areas along the bank edge can eliminate this problem.[74]

in encouraging use of coastal floodplain areas for agriculture, providing proper controls and buffer strips are used, is the prevention of extensive property damage and loss of life from flooding that may occur in urbanized floodway areas.

Conversely, tidelands and wetlands should not be used for agriculture (or aquaculture). This practice is rare in the seacoast, but 10,000 acres of tidelands and wetlands have been diked in southern New Jersey by salt hay farmers.[73] In South Carolina rice is grown behind dikes to attract waterfowl for hunters. The purpose of the dikes is to stabilize the water flow—in New Jersey it is to hold out water and in South

118

Carolina to hold it in. In either case, the dikes adversely obstruct the continuity from the marsh to estuary, blocking the passage of fishes to the marsh, and the flow of nutrients to the estuary. Partially blocked marshes can also become mosquito havens (as in New Jersey), and encourage the application of pesticides. Any alteration of the marsh for agriculture is detrimental to the natural functioning of the ecosystem. For example, if the 10,000 New Jersey acres were restored to natural marsh by removing the dikes, 20,000 clapper rails would be bred there, and 10,000 black ducks would winter there.[73]

Recommended Constraints:

    1. The best existing methods are to be used for control of erosion and runoff contamination by nutrients and toxicants in shoreland agriculture.

    2. Farmlands in the coastal watershed are to be separated from watercourses and shorelines by a buffer strip of natural vegetation of sufficient width to remove significant amounts of pollutants from runoff waters.

    3. Natural drainage patterns are to be maintained; waterflow is not to be impeded by excavation or alteration of land topography.

    4. Contamination from fertilizer and biocide runoff is to be controlled by selection of appropriate products and by correct techniques of application.

    5. Encouragement of agriculture in coastal areas for aesthetic benefit is compatible with protection of coastal ecosystems if appropriate safeguards are taken.

    6. *Vital areas* are not to be preempted for agriculture.

SEPTIC TANKS

Septic tanks and related systems for underground disposal of domestic wastes often are a major source of pollution of coastal waters when they are installed along the shores of water bodies.

The septic tank is a storage chamber for a more complex treatment system in which the actual purification is accomplished within the soils of the drainage field (Figure 62). In low-lying coastal areas, the effluent often leaches through the soil too rapidly. It is inadequately treated when it reaches the water basin and arrives in contaminated condition, polluting the water with bacteria and nutrients. Nitrogen, which is particularly mobile in ground water, is the probable cause of the most adverse estuarine eutrophication (the nitrogen concentration of septic tank effluents may be as high as 5-15 ppm).[75]

Where soil absorption is poor, septic tanks do not drain properly; the

119

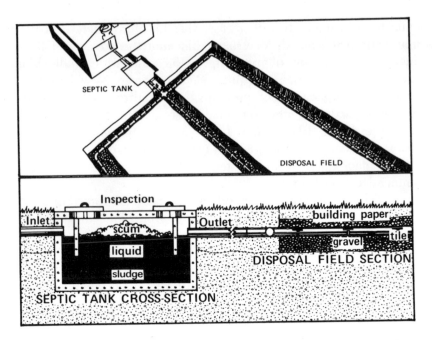

Figure 62. A typical septic tank sewage-disposal system.[76]

liquid waste saturates the soil and then rises to flow over the surface of the ground and into coastal waters. This pollution potential is exacerbated in low-lying coastal areas where high tides and storms raise the water table and saturate the soils.

There are three major potential problems relating to septic tanks in coastal areas: (1) wastes are leached into coastal waters when septic tanks are located too close to the shore, (2) tidally-induced high water tables provide direct and rapid flushing of drain fields into coastal waters and (3) inadequate drain field components or soil absorption characteristics cause tanks to overflow, particularly during rainstorms, and to pollute coastal waters.

These hazards weigh heavily against the use of septic tanks in coastal floodplain areas and for the use of central sewage systems. Where central treatment facilities are not practicable, septic tank and drain field systems are to be replaced, expanded or improved where necessary to insure that overflow to coastal waters does not occur. In no event should overflow pipes be permitted. Periodic removal of sludge and scum will prevent malfunction leading to pollution of coastal waters. The solids removed are to be trucked to treatment facilities. In tidal areas where there is inadequate soil depth over solid rock or clay, or the ground-water table, septic tanks are not to be installed (a four-foot depth is generally required beneath the drainage lines[77]).

Septic tanks installed above the floodplain level need only follow general standards, except on steeply rising shores where precautions are required to prevent leaching of wastes into coastal waters. As a general rule, tanks and drain fields are to be set back a minimum 150 feet from the upper floodplain boundary to prevent BOD and nutrient pollution of coastal waters.

Recommended Constraints:

    1. Septic tanks are not to be used in coastal floodplain areas.

    2. A minimum setback of 150 feet from the upper floodplain boundary is recommended for septic tanks.

    3. Existing systems are to be improved or replaced where necessary to function optimally; regular cleaning is to be enforced.

MUNICIPAL AND PACKAGE SEWAGE TREATMENT FACILITIES

Central sewage treatment facilities have the potential for improvement of the quality of coastal waters if they are properly located, designed and operated. If not, they may only accomplish a transfer of major pollution from dispersed sources to concentrated point sources.

Four major water pollution problems of human waste are: (1) hazard to human health from pathogens (Figure 63), (2) oxygen reduction from BOD loading, (3) eutrophication from dissolved organic and inorganic substances and (4) aesthetic offenses.

The most insidious pollution effect is eutrophication because the typical treatment plant removes no more than half of the high concentrations of phosphate and nitrate nutrient in sewage (Table 7). The effluent is discharged with concentrations of phosphate and nitrate nutrients of 15-50 ppm—which are perhaps 100 to 1,000 times higher than levels in the otherwise healthy coastal waters it may enter.[78] The effect of discharging this treated effluent is to cause eutrophication of poorly flushed estuarine waters, causing high turbidity and oxygen reduction. A typical analysis of secondary treatment effluents is shown in Table 8. Oxygen reduction is a problem in confined estuaries, even when there is secondary treatment of effluents.

The apparent best solution to the oxygen reduction and overfertilization problem is land treatment of the effluent after conventional secondary treatment (or tertiary where necessary). In a properly integrated land use plan, sufficient naturally or artificially vegetated land would be set aside to purify the effluent, removing the organic (BOD) content and the inorganic (phosphate and nitrate) nutrients in passing across vege-

121

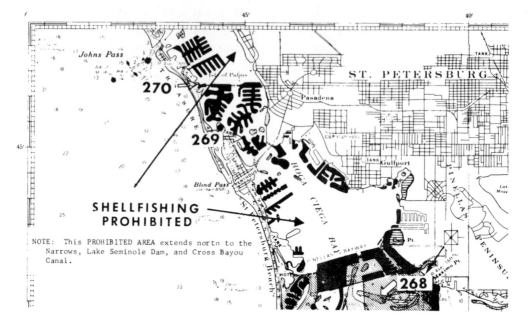

Figure 63. Urban pollution contaminates shellfish beds. (Boca Ciega Bay, Florida.) [63]

tated terrain and through the soils. In an *optimum* system with appropriate slopes (3-6%), and vegetation (e.g., canary grass), 130 acres may handle the wastes of 10,000 people.[80] More than 500 U.S. municipalities use some form of land disposal or treatment of wastes.[80] Golf courses, farms, timber land, or natural meadow and marshland buffer areas can be used for this purpose.

To accomplish this purification effectively, it may be more efficient to plan a number of smaller, strategically located treatment plants, than to go toward fewer, high-capacity, central treatment facilities. Package plants, designed to treat the wastes of small 50 to 150-unit developments, may be particularly amenable to this type of vegetative "polishing." In certain areas the imaginative use of artificial water bodies may provide a method of final polishing of effluents.[81, 43]

A very severe pollution problem occurs when, because of plant malfunction or, more usually, because of overload, a plant's capacity is exceeded and sewage overflows, untreated, to coastal waters. This results in a high degree of pathogen contamination of shellfish, over-fertilization of waters, and oxygen reduction. A frequent cause of overload is heavy rainfall that is directed via storm drains into the sewage plant. The

122

	Removal efficiency of treatment	
	Primary	Primary Plus Secondary
Biochemical oxygen demand	35%	90%
Chemical oxygen demand	30%	80%
Refractory organics	20%	60%
Suspended Solids	60%	90%
Total nitrogen	20%	50%
Total phosphorus	10%	30%
Dissolved minerals	—	5%

Table 7. Average efficiency of primary and secondary sewage treatment plants.[77]

solution is to plan separate treatment facilities for storm runoff waters which are themselves heavily polluted with nutrients, organic waste, oil and other toxic substances.

Because it is most efficient to operate a sewage collection system by gravity flow, coastal treatment plants have often been built in low-lying areas along coastal water courses. The effluent, then, can be simply disposed of into the adjacent waters. The collection trunk mains are often routed through wetlands along the water's edge where inexpensive land is available and where they can flow easily to the treatment plant. These expediencies, which have caused the loss of a great acreage of valuable wetlands and tidelands, are to be discouraged. If the effluent is to be directed upland for vegetative purification before reaching coastal waters, the plants may as well be located at higher elevations themselves. There would be a cost for pumping sewage to the plant but the effluent would then flow by gravity to the vegetated polishing areas and buffer areas.

	Concentration (mg/l)	Average increment added during water use (mg/l)
Gross organics	55	52
BOD & COD	25	25
Sodium	135	70
Potassium	15	10
Ammonium	20	20
Calcium	60	15
Magnesium	25	7
Chloride	130	75
Nitrate	15	10
Bicarbonate	300	100
Sulfate	100	30
Silica	50	15
Phosphate	25	25
Hardness (as calcium carbonate)	270	70
Alkalinity (as calcium carbonate)	250	85
Total dissolved solids	730	320

Table 8. Typical content of secondary treatment effluents (in mg/l).[79]

Recommended Constraints:

1. Land treatment of treated sewage effluent is to be used in preference to discharge into estuarine waters; buffer areas and green areas are to be set aside for vegetative purification of land-disposed effluents.

2. Shoreland sewage system effluents will need pre-treatment to permit land treatment.

3. Treatment plants are not to receive industrial wastes or storm water (except certain ones with ocean outfalls).

4. Sewage systems—mains as well as treatment plants and lagoons—are not to be built in wetland or tideland areas.

SITE PREPARATION

Control of site preparation—land clearing, grading and surfacing—is a basic element of coastal land and water use management. The management framework includes consideration of location, design and construction activity. About one million acres of land are cleared for development each year in the United States and much of this is shoreland.

In summary, uncontrolled site preparation poses the following dangers: *land clearing* increases erosion, causing soil and nutrient pollution, and reduces the stability of water runoff patterns, resulting in adverse alteration of salinity and circulation of coastal waters; *grading* changes land topography and alters surface flow patterns, leading to the same disturbances as land clearing; *surfacing* the land with impervious materials exacerbates runoff flow and pollution problems (page 37).

Disturbances can be minimized first by selective location of development to avoid *vital areas*—wetlands, tidelands and drainageways.

Construction sites have a higher *potential* yield of sediment runoff from erosion than any other major land activity, as shown in the following representative data:[72]

Activity	Sediment Produced (tons/sq. mi./yr.)
Construction	48,000
Cropland	4,800
Grassland	240
Forest	24
Disturbed Forest (not clear-cut)	24,000
Active Surface Mines	24,000
Abandoned Mines	2,400

Erosion prevention methods in the coastal watershed should be based on the following standard principles: (1) fitting development plans to climatic factors, topography, soils and vegetative cover; (2) reducing the area and the duration of exposed soils; (3) retaining a maximum of natural vegetation; (4) covering disturbed soils with mulch or vegetation; and (5) retarding runoff and erosion with intercepting barriers.

Methods consistent with these principles include: (1) thorough site planning with the aid of a geologist or soil scientist; (2) exposing soils only as needed for immediate development and roughening the surface of exposed banks to decrease runoff and slow downhill soil movement; (3) planting fast growing annual and perennial plants to cover denuded areas; (4) using natural plant mulches, chemical soil stabilizers, fiber mulches or netting to cover the soil; and (5) building soil or stone dikes, ditches and terraces to intercept runoff and divert it from erodible soil.

The configuration of design grades should be planned to respect the existing natural pattern of surface water flow to the maximum extent possible rather than shortcircuiting flows to simplify drainage. The natural pattern will ordinarily direct runoff water through vegetated areas and soils thereby guaranteeing stability of flows and the maximum of natural removal of pollutants (page 42).

Additional safeguards, required during the construction phase, may include the following: (1) gravel inlet filters, consisting of stone or gravel placed around or in front of an inlet to a drainage channel; (2) sediment traps, built of straw bales, sandbags, or stones placed across small drainageways; (3) sediment basins, designed to hold stormwater, temporarily detain runoff and allow time for settling of sediment; and (4) diversion structures—dikes, ditches and terraces.[95]

In the design phase, general control practices involve planning for vegetative buffer areas to filter and detain the movement of runoff water, thereby slowing the transport of soil. Buffer area control practices include leaving natural vegetation between sediment sources and waterways or designing buffer areas into artificial landscapes.

A solution to disturbances from impervious surfaces is to substitute porous surface materials wherever possible, such as gravel instead of concrete for driveways and parking lots. In addition, all non-substitutable impervious area that might drain into confined coastal waters is to be properly drained and connected to a storm water collection and treatment system (page 40).

Recommended Constraints:

1. The best available erosion and sedimentation control methods are to be used in coastal watersheds.

2. Final grades are to be designed to facilitate drainage by the original natural patterns.

3. Impervious surfaces are to be kept to the minimum; porous materials are to be substituted to the maximum extent possible.

4. Natural vegetation is to be preserved to the maximum to retain the natural volume and periodicity of runoff flow.

5. Buffer strips are to be incorporated between developed areas and all watercourses to mitigate persistent washoff of pollutants.

ROADWAYS

In the absence of environmental safeguards, coastal area roadways not only alter the lands of the road right-of-way but induce new forms of land use along the road corridor and, through pollution and physical disruption, reduce the quality of coastal ecosystems. To reduce adverse impacts it is necessary to identify and control sources of environmental disturbance during all stages of highway planning, construction and maintenance.

Location is the most critical aspect of roadway planning. Roadways should not be located in *vital areas*. Nor should they impinge on *areas of environmental concern* except under strict environmental constraints. The nearer a roadway is to water, the greater is its pollution potential (Figure 64). The coastal floodplain is usually an inappropriate location for a major highway. Those with unrestricted access and an extensive induced development corridor are particularly inappropriate.

The disturbances from highway construction in wetlands have been serious. The removal of unsuitable marsh soils to reach a stable substrate has required extensive excavation and problems with disposal of the overburden, or spoil. If placed in wetlands areas, the spoil pre-empts marsh habitat, releases toxic substances, and depletes oxygen in the water. Soil discharge into waterways causes turbidity which reduces biological productivity and causes siltation of water bodies (page 21). Roads built on solid fill causeways become dams that block natural water flow and degrade wetlands. Important sections of estuarine environment can be converted to polluted impoundments as a result of being cut off from tidal water flow by highway fill. Essential feeder roadways that must cross wetlands should be elevated to eliminate these adverse effects (see page 129).

The ecological precept that water flow must not be obstructed is a governing factor in the location and design of road systems in coastal areas (page 16). The general flow of water is perpendicular to the coast and structures built parallel to the coast tend to block flow. Therefore, major highways should not be located in the floodplain parallel to the coast where they intercept freshwater flow to ecologically valuable wetlands and tidelands or across estuaries where they prevent tidal flushing. A highway should not be located parallel to beaches exposed to storm waves or proximal to dunes which shift with winds and storm waves.

127

Figure 64. Improperly located roadways lead to deterioration of dunelines.

Feeder roads should be perpendicular to the coastline and not across the path of either freshwater flow or tidewater movement. Only essential service roads that must run parallel to the coast should be permitted and these are to be provided with sufficient water passes and culverts to provide as near a natural pattern of runoff and tidal flow as possible. Bridges and pile-supported causeways can be incorporated into the design plan to reduce interference with tidal creeks, overland flow and natural transport of sand along shore (page 129).

Control of roadway construction, operation and maintenance activities is needed to prevent erosion and sedimentation, obstruction of ground-water recharge, alteration of stream flow and salinity levels and increased pollution and eutrophication of coastal waters. Construction activities of concern are excavation for borrow material, cuts and fills, land clearing, grading and recontouring, and stream channelization or realignment.

Effects related to day-to-day use and maintenance of roadways are usually of secondary impact but can be significant in certain situations. Continuing disturbances occur from: altered runoff from road surfaces and improperly graded or vegetated adjacent slopes, soil erosion and the

128

introduction of de-icing salts, herbicides and runoff of street surface contaminants into nearby watercourses.

Recommended Constraints:

1. Major roadways are to be located above the coastal floodplain.

2. Roadways built in coastal watersheds shall be designed and located so as to prevent pollution of runoff water or interference with natural drainage patterns.

3. Major roadways within the coastal floodplain are to be located parallel to land drainage flow (generally, perpendicular to the coast).

4. Essential minor roadways are to be designed to facilitate the flow of land drainage and coastal waters.

5. Essential wetland, tideland, and estuarine crossings are to be built as elevated structures.

BRIDGES AND CAUSEWAYS

Bridges and causeways have a potential for interference with patterns of water flow in tidal areas and for preemption and disturbance of *vital areas.* Hence, it is advisable to locate major roadways above the coastal floodplain, so that the need for bridges and causeways across wetlands, tidelands and water basins is reduced.

Bridges should be designed so as not to impair tidal flow—volume, velocity or direction. Most simply, the cross sectional area of a watercourse is not to be reduced by abutments, support piers, pilings, etc. Abutments should be built back from the water edge and clear spans used rather than piers if feasible. It may be necessary at times to enlarge the watercourse before construction in order to finish with the original cross sectional area. The same general principal—non-reduction of watercourse cross-section—applies to use of culverts to allow passage of flow under roadways.

Where it is imperative to plan a roadway through a wetland, tideland, or open area, the roadbed is to be elevated by the use of pile supports rather than fill. A solid fill causeway has a potential for serious blockage of flow (Figure 65). Also, solid fill construction usually requires extensive dredging for fill and excavation of construction access canals which results in additional loss of wetlands and tidelands, soil discharge into the estuary, disruption of waterflows, etc. (page 101). Construction should be segmental (or end-on), which is somewhat more costly than the standard method, but it avoids the need for damaging canal excavation (Figure 66).

129

Figure 65. Solid fill causeway crossings impede estuarine circulation and lead to ecosystem degradation.

Recommended Constraints:

     1. Bridge structures are to be designed so as not to impede or reduce the natural volume or rate of flow of water.

     2. Causeways through wetlands, tidelands or estuarine basins are to be elevated with piers or pilings rather than fill, and segmental construction is to be used.

     3. Extreme care is to be taken to reduce soil discharge and other disturbances during highway construction.

ELECTRIC POWER PLANTS

In the construction phase, power plants have the potential for such environmental disturbances as soil discharge, disruption of marshes and tidal flats and disruption of water flow in tidelands. This potential for environmental disturbance is similar to many other large-scale industrial

130

Figure 66. Modern methods of bridge construction avoid adverse eco-system disturbances caused by access canal dredging (Michael Fahey, Sandy Hook Marine Laboratory).

developments in coastal shorelands and all appropriate construction safeguards are required.

Broad estuarine marshscapes offer particularly attractive sites for nuclear plants, because the price of marshland is low, cooling water is available and a high degree of seclusion is possible. However, this con-

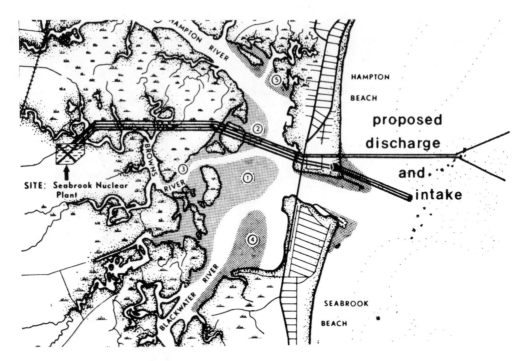

Figure 67. The initial plan for the Seabrook-Hampton Power Plant (N. H.).

flicts with state and national initiatives for protection of these vital areas (Figure 67). Power plants are to be sited so that no preemption or alteration of *vital areas* occurs (Figure 68). Disruption of coastal waters must also be avoided such as that described below by C. C. Coutant: [83]

> ... Dredging for an intake channel or discharge pipeline is the construction activity which can have the greatest impact on aquatic biota. Removing sediments from fresh and salt water is known to have potential for biological damage to populations (1) in the immediate areas of dredging (by disruption of bottom organisms and their habitat); (2) in areas of intentional disposal of dredged materials (by covering existing bottom organisms and modifying habitats); and (3) in unexpected areas within the general region where water quality may be altered (increased turbidity, reduction in quantity of dissolved oxygen due to suspension of oxygen-demanding sediments, release of toxic materials, etc.) or bottom organisms are covered by a smothering siltation.

In the operating phase, steam electric plants pose a special and unique set of continuing disturbances to coastal water environments whether

132

Figure 68. Unfortunate installation of spray canal system at Pittsburg steam plant (Sacramento-San Joaquin delta, California) that has pre-empted and severely disrupted an environmentally critical shore area. (Courtesy: P.G.&E., San Francisco, Calif.) [18]

they are fueled by oil, coal, or nuclear energy. With a typical modern nuclear plant of 1,000 megawatts capacity fitted with open cycle cooling, water goes through the plant in less than one minute and its temperature is raised by 10 to 34°F (6° to 19°C) before being discharged directly back to public waters (Figure 69). The resulting thermal pollution has adverse effects on aquatic life. There are also effects of varying extent from toxic chemical pollutants added to the cooling water—these discharges are governed by Federal law and implemented by joint Federal-state programs.

It must be made clear that thermal discharges are not usually the major source of disturbance caused by coastal steam plants. The major disturbance is associated with *entrainment*, whereby multitudes of aquatic forms are drawn in with the cooling water and killed within the plant by heat, turbulence, abrasion and shock (Figure 70). The effects

133

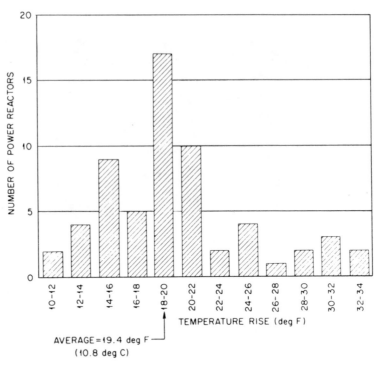

Figure 69. Design temperature rises through condensers of 67 nuclear power plants.[84]

are especially direct and severe with plants located on estuarine spawning and nursery areas of fish and shellfish. In these areas, stratified water circulation, coupled with natural behavior aspects of species, cause suspended organisms to be exposed to entrainment over and over as they repeatedly cycle past a steam plant. For example, up to 30 percent or more of the annual brood of an estuarine-spawning fish can be killed by the operation of one 1,000 megawatt plant located in a breeding *vital area,* such as the Indian Point plant on the Hudson Estuary.[85] In this same area, Consolidated Edison has planned a large *pump-storage plant* that would pump up to 1.7 billion cubic feet of water per day from the estuary and potentially eliminate 25-75 percent of the young striped bass of each year's brood.[86] There is no specific Federal law to control entrainment and each case is considered on its separate merits by Federal authorities under provision of such laws as the Rivers and Harbors Act of 1899 or the National Environmental Policy Act of 1969.

Thermal pollution from power plants acts to change the natural patterns of life and behavior of all aquatic species. How pervasive this may be and how damaging depends upon the volume of public water basin that is polluted and its flushing characteristics. For example, the

134

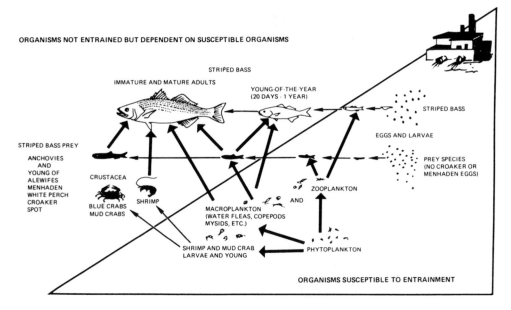

ORGANISMS NOT ENTRAINED BUT DEPENDENT ON SUSCEPTIBLE ORGANISMS

STRIPED BASS
IMMATURE AND MATURE ADULTS

YOUNG-OF-THE-YEAR
(20 DAYS - 1 YEAR)

STRIPED BASS

EGGS AND LARVAE

STRIPED BASS PREY

ANCHOVIES
AND
YOUNG OF
ALEWIFES
MENHADEN
WHITE PERCH
CROAKER
SPOT

PREY SPECIES
(NO CROAKER OR
MENHADEN EGGS)

CRUSTACEA

ZOOPLANKTON

SHRIMP   AND

BLUE CRABS
MUD CRABS

MACROPLANKTON
(WATER FLEAS, COPEPODS
MYSIDS, ETC.)

SHRIMP AND MUD CRAB   PHYTOPLANKTON
LARVAE AND YOUNG

ORGANISMS SUSCEPTIBLE TO ENTRAINMENT

Figure 70. Diagram shows areas of potential power plant impact on striped bass and associated food items.[87]

Hudson Estuary temperature would be raised by 4 to 5°F (2 - 3°C) over a reach of 35 miles by 5 assorted plants, a sufficient rise to kill delicate striped bass at certain embryonic stages and increase abundance of undesirable blue-green algae[18] (Figure 71). Where water is shallow and protected by sand bars, such as in the sheltered coast of West Florida (Figure 72), grass beds can be extensively damaged by temperature buildup from thermal pollution. Thermal discharges also disturb the behavior of marine species; for example, where the warm water sinks in the inner, low-salinity parts of northern estuaries in winter (with estuary temperatures near freezing), fishes are attracted toward the plant from their deep winter areas where they are killed on the screens that protect the intake pump of the cooling water system (Figure 73). In this fashion, about one million fish per year are killed on the screens of a small (290 mw^e) steam plant at Indian Point on the Hudson Estuary (N.Y.) each winter.

From a general ecosystems aspect, the effects of thermal pollution are integrated through a wide series of effects and interactions such as the following:[3]

    1. Heat affects the physical properties of water such as density, viscosity, vapor pressure and solubility of dissolved gases. Consequently, such processes as the settling

135

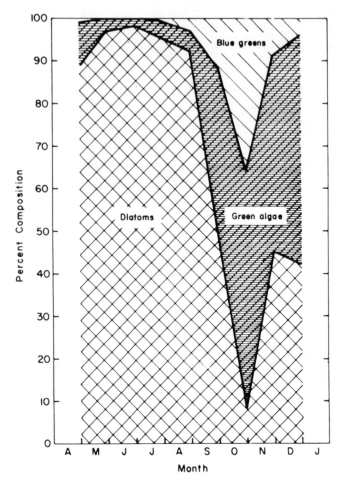

Figure 71. High water temperature decrease beneficial diatoms and increase detrimental blue-green algae as shown by the change in relative proportions of diatoms.[85]

of particulate matter, stratification, circulation and evaporation can be influenced by changes in temperature. Since the solubility of oxygen in water decreases as temperature increases, thermal pollution reduces the oxygen resources.

2. Heat affects the rate at which chemical reactions progress, and it can speed up the formation of undesirable compounds or change dynamic chemical equilibria. It also affects biochemical reactions and can result in a more rapid depletion of the oxygen resources.

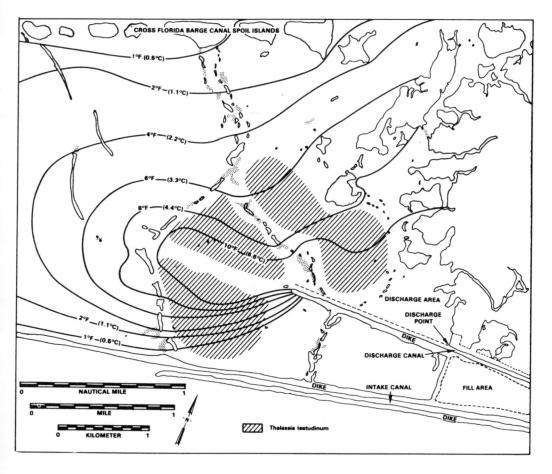

Figure 72. Predicted temperature increments above ambient (at 3 feet below the surface, average for full tidal cycle) for a power plant at Crystal River, Florida (shaded areas are grass beds).[88]

3. Physiological processes such as reproduction, development and metabolism are temperature dependent. The range of many species of fishes and the species composition of communities are governed to a great extent by the environmental temperature. Temperature anomalies also can block the passage of anadromous fish, greatly reducing future populations.

4. Thermal pollution affects other aquatic organisms such as the aquatic plants, the benthos and the bacterial populations. Increased temperatures may reduce the numbers of species in the community and stimulate excessive

137

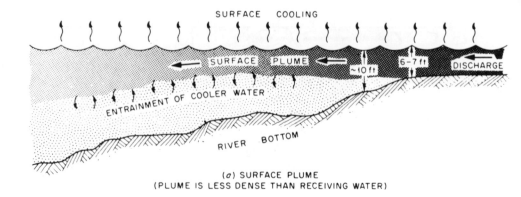

(a) SURFACE PLUME
(PLUME IS LESS DENSE THAN RECEIVING WATER)

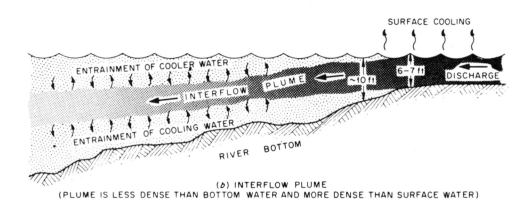

(b) INTERFLOW PLUME
(PLUME IS LESS DENSE THAN BOTTOM WATER AND MORE DENSE THAN SURFACE WATER)

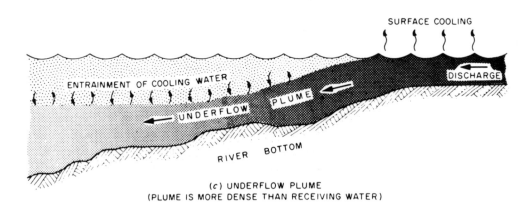

(c) UNDERFLOW PLUME
(PLUME IS MORE DENSE THAN RECEIVING WATER)

Figure 73. Discharge plume conditions for a low salinity upper estuary in northern latitudes.[89]

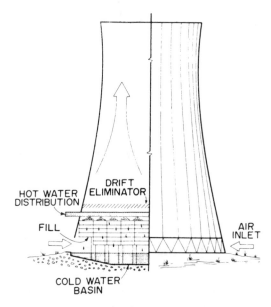

Figure 74. Natural draft wet cooling tower for power plant closed cycle condenser cooling.[90]

populations of individual species to nuisance conditions.

The solution to the power plant problem lies in appropriate site selection and in proper design of the cooling system. Estuaries are *areas of environmental concern* and plants may be located on them only if they are equipped with *closed cycle* cooling systems such as properly placed spray canals or cooling towers (Figures 74 and 68), where the discharge water is continuously cooled by evaporation, is recycled through the condensers and, consequently, does not require the massive withdrawal of water that characterizes *open cycle* cooling. With the closed-cycle safeguard, adverse effects on aquatic life can be reduced to an acceptable level in most cases. However, an ecological survey must precede any site selection action, so that all *vital areas* may be identified and exempted as sites for power plants regardless of cooling system.

Although ecologically safer, cooling towers may still be unacceptable from an aesthetic viewpoint because of their height, form and vapor plume. But the spray canal system of closed-cycle cooling obviates most of the aesthetic problems and may be used wherever meteorological conditions are favorable for its mode of operation.

Recommended Constraints:

1. Wetlands, tidelands, and other *vital areas* are inappropriate sites for power plants.

139

2. Open-cycle cooling is acceptable only for open coast or offshore ocean sites, away from *areas of environmental concern,* and then only if appropriate safeguards are employed in design of the cooling water system and the location of intakes and outlets.

3. Closed-cycle cooling is required for all power plants located on or adjacent to estuaries, bays, lagoons and other *areas of environmental concern.*

4. Power plants are not to be located on, or adjacent to, *vital areas* regardless of cooling system—and these areas are to be delineated in biotic surveys and set aside as zones of exclusion for power plants and other installations with a similar potential environmental disturbance.

URBAN RUNOFF

Runoff from urbanized areas has serious adverse effects on the quality of coastal waters. The average acre of land in the United States receives about one million gallons of precipitation each year. Around one third of this goes off to the atmosphere in evaporation and transpiration. The remainder finds its way to a watercourse and thence to the sea. Coastal waters are strongly influenced by this runoff and by its content and rate of discharge. The sources of runoff contamination are exemplified below (for Gainesville, Florida):[91]

Air Pollution: fallout of particles, rainout of particles and gases.

Street Litter: material that accumulates in streets and parking lots which can be removed by sweeping.

Yard Refuse: leaves, grass, limbs, etc.

Septic Tanks, Privies: flushing of soil by rain or flooding by storms.

Inactive Garbage Dumps: old inactive dumps, especially for private purposes, that may still contribute organic matter.

Improper Garbage Handling: exposure to rain before pickup or improperly distributed on land.

Stagnant Water: in containers, low areas, and specifically in catch basins along street.

Poorly Paved Streets: that disintegrate and contribute silt during rains. Also includes heavily oiled unpaved surfaces for dust control.

Car Washing: including soap and dirt from vehicle and other outdoor cleaning activities.

140

Fuel, Chemical Spillage: from bulk storage and handling.
Lawn Sprinkling: loosens dirt and washes down fertilizers and pesticides.
Vehicle Drippings: gasoline, oils, brake fluid, and other material. Includes deliberate hosing of service station areas.
Commercial and Industrial: exposed trash piles or contaminated surfaces.
Construction and Maintenance: exposed dirt piles, debris, materials, etc.
Insect Spraying Programs: mosquito control.
Home Gardening: exposed soil, pesticides, and fertilizers.
Illicit Dumping: of any foreign substance deliberately poured into street.

Water draining from natural terrain passes over vegetated land as overland flow or through the soil as ground water flow. In either case it receives highly effective natural purification treatment. Pollutants are removed biologically by microorganisms or plants; or physically by filtration, absorption or deposition; or chemically by oxidation and other reactions. Purification continues in the streams and other natural flow-ways by the same processes. Natural flow-ways tend to meander through coastal plains areas thus slowing passage of water to the sea and allowing greater opportunity for natural purification. Meandering water courses are also conducive to streamside vegetation which aids greatly in purification.

Any change in the natural pattern of land drainage must be presumed to have adverse effects on water quality including: filling or devegetation of drainageways, alteration of natural land grades, straightening or channelization of watercourses, land clearing, land surfacing and so forth (page 40). Therefore, shoreland management should respect the principle of retaining the system of land drainage as near to the natural pattern as possible (page 42).

The typical storm drainage system is designed to short circuit the natural process. Runoff water is diverted to street drains and thence to collection pipes, trunks and to an outlet which discharges into the nearest watercourse. Alternatively the system is combined with the sewers and storm water is carried to the sewage treatment plant. In either case, all possibility for purification and holdback of storm water by natural process is foregone. The result is serious disturbance of the coastal water ecosystem.

The pollution effects from storm drain discharges can be mitigated to a degree by installing a treatment plant to remove contaminants—this may be required by the 1972 Federal Water Act Amendments aimed at elimi-

	STREET SURFACE RUNOFF (following 1 hr storm) (lb/hr)	RAW SANITARY SEWAGE (lb/hr)	SECONDARY PLANT EFFLUENT (lb/hr)
Settleable plus Suspended Solids	560,000	1,300	130
BOD_5	5,600	1,100	110
COD	13,000	1,200	120
Kjeldahl nitrogen	800	210	20
Phosphates	440	50	2.5
Total cell form bacteria (org/hr)	4000×10^{10}	$460,000 \times 10^{10}$	4.6×10^{10}

Table 9. Calculated quantities of pollutants which would enter receiving waters (hypothetical city: streets = 4,000 curb miles, cleaned each 5 days; pop. = 100,000; area = 14,000 acres, 75% resid., 5% comml., 20% industr.; sewage = 12 million g.p.d.).[92]

nating pollution discharges into public waters.[29] Storm runoff waters from urban areas may contain higher concentrations of various pollutants than raw sewage, as shown in Table 9. Because urban runoff flow is sporadic, an efficient treatment system requires high storage capacity in order to avoid building the huge capacity plant required to treat peak runoff flows spontaneously.

Combining the storm drain and sewage systems for convenience and economy is not usually acceptable because existing combined systems are generally not capable of handling the combined load during runoff surges. A treatment plant of sufficient capacity to handle the peak storm flow along with the sewage load might be uneconomic. Also, the treatment required for sewage would be quite different than that required for storm water because the contaminant concentration is so different (see Table 9). The appropriate solution is to separate the two functions and optimize each for its specific purpose.

For protection of coastal waters the best storm drain system is one which most nearly simulates the natural system; that is, one that has features to hold back storm runoff and to provide the maximum of natural purification. The ideal would be to preserve and utilize existing natural drainageways—creeks, sloughs, swales and so forth. Land preparation for development would include grading requirements to enhance natural-type flow. Runoff waters from the developed areas would be diverted through areas of natural soils and vegetation into natural drainageways. Porous paving materials and french drains would be used to reduce the amount of surface runoff.[93] Prevention campaigns or regulations would be used to reduce the source amounts (page 113). Such a system could function without a storm water treatment facility in a coastal community of moderate density if it was included in the original planning.[81] In more densely developed communities it might be necessary to incorporate impoundments or ponding areas into the system to make up for the reduced natural storage capacity caused by devegetation, paving and rooftops.[94] The natural system would function very effectively and virtually cost free in a coastal community set back from the water's edge by a vegetated buffer area which would serve as the natural filter and runoff purifier between the community and the coastal waters.

Communities that are already in advanced development may find a partial solution in diverting storm runoff through remaining natural areas of appropriate slope and soil type where natural purification can take place. If the appropriate natural conditions do not prevail, it is possible to design and construct a sloped and vegetated surface for efficient land treatment.[80]

The goal of the drainage system should be to control runoff water quality so that, when discharged to public waters, it is as near its natural condition as possible. This will require removal of sediment, toxic contaminants, human pathogens, substances that remove oxygen (BOD) and nutrients. It is especially important to remove nitrogenous wastes because they cause eutrophication of coastal waters and the numerous adverse impacts which follow (page 19).

Recommended Constraints:

1. Urban runoff is not to be discharged directly to coastal waters.

2. Development in coastal areas is to be planned to leave the natural system of land drainage intact and to provide for natural treatment by soil filtration and vegetative purification.

3. Where natural treatment is not possible, runoff is to be artificially stored to control its rate of discharge and restored by treatment to as near natural quality as possible.

4. In most cases it is necessary to separate storm drain systems from municipal sewage systems to provide the most efficient treatment for both.

5. Impervious surface is to be minimized.

6. Natural streamcourses are not to be channeled, straightened or otherwise modified.

WATER CONTROL STRUCTURES

Management of coastal ecosystems is largely a process of maintaining the natural water regime, particularly those aspects relating to the fresh water supply, a dominant ecological influence in the estuarine environment (page 4). To accomplish this, a number of water-related controls on development in shorelands are required, as discussed elsewhere in this guidebook (page 125). However, management of water supply to coastal basins must often extend upstream, out of the coastal district. Water control structures—dams, diversions, impoundments—are of particular concern.

Through altering the amount and rate of flow of the fresh water supply, these structures strongly influence the salinity of coastal waters. A long term *net reduction* in fresh water essentially shrinks the most productive part of the estuary, the brackish middle to upper part (page 15), and may seriously reduce its capacity to support life. A significant change in the *natural rhythm of flow* disrupts critical salinity-related functions of the species that are tuned to this rhythm; such as breeding, migration, defense against predators and feeding. In short, the estuarine ecosystem is closely tuned to a certain salinity pattern that should be maintained by effective management of fresh water inflow.

A significant reduction in fresh water supply may seriously degrade the coastal ecosystem by altering circulation and reducing flushing rate (page 37) or reduce the natural supply of nutrient (page 38). River structures may block the migration routes of anadromous fishes (seafish that spawn in rivers), and seriously interfere with their breeding potential. A problem of growing impact is the diversion of water from breeding areas of fish like striped bass whose larval and juvenile stages live suspended in the river water for many weeks. If a significant proportion of the water is removed, taking with it the suspended fish, there will be a significant reduction of breeding potential (page 133). Diversion of water from the Sacramento River is a likely cause of a 50 percent reduction during the 1960's in San Francisco Bay striped bass.[23] Similarly, diversion of Hudson River water by the proposed Storm King pump storage plant is predicted to reduce striped bass of the Hudson stock by 25 to 75 percent.[86]

Control of fresh water supply from outside the coastal district requires activity on a regional scale and input to the assessment of the impacts of upstream water control projects as they affect coastal ecosystems. Recommended Constraints:

  1. The effects on coastal ecosystems must be included in assessments of the impact of "upstream" water control and diversion projects.
  2. The flow of fresh water into coastal basins is not to be significantly changed by water diversion or water control projects.
  3. Water withdrawal from *vital areas* of the coastal ecosystem is to be prevented.

MOSQUITO CONTROL*

The five dominant U.S. salt marsh mosquito species share the same basic life history and ecology. Eggs are laid singly on the moist, organic soil of the marsh, seldom where there is no vegetative cover and never on free water. In a few days the fully-developed larva is ready to hatch but will do so only when covered by tide or rain water. After hatching (7 to 15 days at summer temperatures) the newly-emerged females mate, feed on nectar, disperse widely, then start biting (blood being necessary for ovarian development) and laying the eggs.

The salt marshes of America are characterized by different plants [96] but, with respect to mosquito ecology, the salient points are that there is a low marsh (tidelands) and a high marsh (wetlands) and that periodicity of submergence varies over the marsh profile; the low marsh is flooded by tide almost daily. Salt marsh mosquitoes cannot breed under the conditions of daily tide floodings on the low marsh, while the high marsh is their domain par excellence where tide floodings with retention of water in depressions for many days produce mosquitoes.

Immobilizing salt marshes [97] with indiscriminate ditching [98] is not an answer. Nor is the use of DDT as a larvicide. The correct method of mosquito control is *open marsh water management,*[99] where ditches are dug only where needed to connect mosquito breeding depressions to tidewater or to ponds, while permanent ponds and pools are saved and isolated from the ditching system. This is expensive, requiring a great deal of preliminary inspection and engineering, but it effectively controls mosquito breeding while interfering least with normal marsh function.[100, 101] It maximizes the effectiveness of mosquito-eating minnows (killifish, mosquito fish, etc.) and facilitates the transport of life forms and nutrients between marsh and estuary. This management method is

*Adapted from an unpublished manuscript by M. W. Provost. Florida Medical Entomology Laboratory, Vero Beach, Florida

145

feasible now through the grass salt marshes of America but its technology has yet to be adapted to the scrub and mangrove tidelands of Florida.[102] Dragline ditching of salt marshes is a well-developed procedure that need not ever, of itself, harm estuaries.

Impounding and flooding salt marshes has been practiced for waterfowl, muskrat and other wildlife management purposes in many states, but its benefits to mosquito control are only incidental, however real. Impounding for mosquito breeding reduction is practiced mostly in Florida, where it also enhances bird abundance.[103] Marshes should be impounded only during the breeding season (warm months) and let tidewater circulate freely otherwise.[104] Mosquito control by impoundment should be limited to tidelands with insufficient tide interval to properly energize a ditching system.

The use of biocides is reserved for and is limited to use of ecologically benign products such as "Abate."

Recommended Constraints:

1. Mosquito reduction is to be accomplished by control of the periodicity of flooding through "open marsh water control".
2. Use of biocides is to be restricted to application of ecologically benign compounds during emergency outbreaks.
3. Indiscriminate ditching of marshland for mosquito control is unacceptable.

DREDGING

Dredging has a high potential for adverse effects on coastal ecosystems.[109] Channels, canals, and ditches—for boat traffic, inland or wetland drainage, and shoreland construction—alter natural water flow patterns, preempt *vital areas,* and pollute coastal waters [110] (page 101).

Dredging creates complex management problems, the solutions to which lie in correct choices of location, design and performance controls. But first, each project should meet a rigorous test of public need because the potential of ecological damage to coastal waters is so high. Large tax-supported dredging projects are popular items for which public need justification is often marginal at best. Private filling of wetlands and tidelands for real estate has, until recently, been approved without public need justification.

Dredging is performed by various types of equipment and methods of operation. Five main types of dredges—both *mechanical* and *hydraulic*—are listed and described in Table 10 (Figure 75). Effective management strategy involves choosing the dredge which, for the job at hand, produces the least ecosystem disturbance.

146

Dipper Dredge—The dipper dredge is basically a power shovel mounted on a barge. the barge (which serves as the work platform for the shovel) uses three spuds (two spuds at the forward end and a single spud at the stern) to provide stability during dredging operations. The dipper dredge is capable of excavating from 3 to 10 cubic yards of hard material per cycle. It can remove blasted rock or loose boulders. The dredged material is discharged within the reach of the dipper boom. The digging boom limits the depth of excavation to not more than 60 feet.

Ladder Dredge—The ladder dredge uses an endless chain of buckets for excavation. The dredge is mounted on a barge which is stabilized by side cables during the dredging operation. The ladder dredge is capable of excavating from 1 to 2 cubic yards of hard material per bucket. It can remove blasted rock or loose boulders. The excavated material is dumped from the buckets into chutes or onto belts and is discharged over the side of the barge. The design of the ladder limits the depth of excavation to not more than 100 feet.

Bucket Dredge—The bucket dredge is basically a crane mounted on a barge. The bucket (clamshell, orange-peel, or dragline) can be changed to suit the job conditions and material to be removed. The barge (which serves as the work platform for the crane) uses either spuds or anchor lines to provide stability during dredging operations. The bucket dredge is capable of excavating moderately stiff material in confined areas. It is generally not used for large scale projects. The excavated material is dumped within the reach of the boom.

Pipeline Dredge—The pipeline dredge is the most versatile and widely used dredge. It can handle large volumes of material in an economical fashion. Using a cutterhead the dredge can excavate material ranging from light silts to heavy rock. It can pump the dredged material through floating and shore discharge lines to remote disposal areas. Pipeline dredges range in sizes (as measured by the diameter of the pump discharge) from 6 inches to 36 inches. The depth of excavation is limited to 60 feet. The rate of dredging will decrease with (1) difficulty in digging, (2) increase in length of discharge pipe and (3) increase in lift to discharge elevation.

Hopper Dredge—The hopper dredge is a self-propelled vessel designed to dredge material hydraulically, to load and retain dredge spoil in hoppers, and then to haul the spoil to a disposal area or dump. Loading is accomplished by sucking the bottom material through a drag-head into the hoppers while making a cut through the dredging area. The quantity of volume pumped during a loading operation depends primarily upon the character of the material and the amount of pumping time involved as well as the hopper capacity and the pumping and propulsive capability of the dredge. The loaded dredge proceeds to the disposal area where the dredge spoil is discharged through gates in the bottom of the hoppers.

Table 10. Five common types of dredge rigs; the first three (dipper, ladder, bucket) are *mechanical dredges,* the last two (pipeline, hopper) are *hydraulic dredges.*[111]

The hydraulic dredge, commonly used in dredging navigation channels, causes the least disturbance from release of polluting sediments at the site of dredging. But it has a high potential for ecologic disturbance at the outlet of the pipeline where the *spoil* (a slurry of sediment and water) is discharged, particularly if it contains a high proportion of polluting materials: organic matter, toxics, fine sediments. Spoil is not to be deposited on *vital areas*—wetlands, tidelands, shellfish beds, etc.—nor

Figure 75. A typical pipeline dredge in operation.

dumped on the bottoms of estuaries (except under certain prescribed conditions discussed later), because of the obliteration of ecologically critical area.

A particularly damaging approach to disposal is to broadcast spoil into coastal waters. Two such approaches used in navigational channel dredging that are unacceptable, and nearly outmoded, are: (1) *sidecast disposal* in which the spoil from a pipeline dredge is discharged directly overboard at the dredge site and (2) the related process of *agitation dredging* whereby the spoil from a hopper dredge is broadcast directly into the water so as to be dispersed widely by current action.[111] Such *overboard discharge* methods cause pervasive pollution when the spoil is from soft bottoms. Where the bottom is coarse and clean—that is, sand or gravel without much clay, mud or organic matter—overboard disposal may be acceptable, providing the spoils are not deposited in banks that significantly impede water flow (page 102). Also there may be positive uses for such clean spoil in public projects such as beach restoration. But

148

Figure 76. Turbidity screens and other silt trapping devices have often proved ineffective in Florida, as illustrated by the turbidity cloud moving unhindered (from left to right) through a screen with water currents. (E. T. LaRoe).

definitely, underwater strip mining should not be permitted in most estuaries simply to obtain sand or gravel for construction materials because of the potential for environmental damage—pollution, disruption of circulation, dredgehole stagnation, etc. (page 152).

There are two reasonable alternatives to overboard release or placement of spoil on estuarine bottoms by pipeline dredges. The first is to use the spoil to build habitat—marshes against the shore, or islands in open estuarine waters—and confine the spoil with levees of material which would degrade in time to leave natural edges. Devices such as turbidity screens or "diaper" silt traps are not a substitute for other safeguards because their function can too easily be: (1) voided by tides, currents and winds which dislocate screens or (2) subverted by uncooperative dredge operators (Figure 76).

The second recommended solution is to dispose of the spoil in a place that is not an estuarine *area of ecological concern*—e.g., inland above the floodplain or in the ocean away from inlets or *vital areas*. Either of these may raise costs to a prohibitive level. Pumping spoil inland requires both the installation of an unwelcome overland pipeline and a complex procedure to de-water the spoil and dispose of the contaminated wastewater (the slurry contains around 75 percent water). The strategy of dumping spoil offshore is also complicated by varying oceanographic factors—currents, depths, stratification of water—and by the widely varying composition of spoils. Ocean disposal is controlled by joint Federal/state authority under the 1972 U.S. Water Act Amendments,[29] and virtually all disposal requires Federal authorization by permit from the Corps of Engineers, with Environmental Protection Agency endorsement.

Navigation channels through coastal waters should be located so as to avoid *vital areas*—tidelands, shellfish beds, grass beds, etc. They should be excavated no deeper than is absolutely necessary—less than 10 feet is preferable [108]—so as to enable bottom plants to receive sunlight and prosper. Also, deeper channels must be redredged more often, increasing costs, ecological disturbance and, at times, increasing habor sedimentation by increasing the inward flow of water along the bottom and therefore the inward transport of materials from the ocean, as happened in the case of Savannah Harbor.[109]

The initial cut of the channel sides is to be at the full expected equilibrium slope to prevent later slumping, resuspension of the sediments, continued unsuitable conditions for bottom plants and animals, as well as the need for redredging. Slopes should normally be greater than 1:5 for sand and 1:10 for mud bottom. Channels should not be located so close to shorelines that there is any danger of perturbing the equilibrium of the natural slope of the bottom and causing erosion of the shore (Figure 77).[44]

Mechanical dredges are used in the coastal zone mostly for onshore or along shore work, such as access canals, marsh drainage, and land filling. Over the years much of this work has been done in ecologically critical areas and there has been an unfortunate loss of *vital area* and damage to *areas of environmental concern* (page   91). This type of activity is to be sharply curtailed or eliminated depending upon the degree of legitimate public need. The ecologic health of the estuarine ecosystem is dependent on keeping critical wetland and tideland areas intact and

150

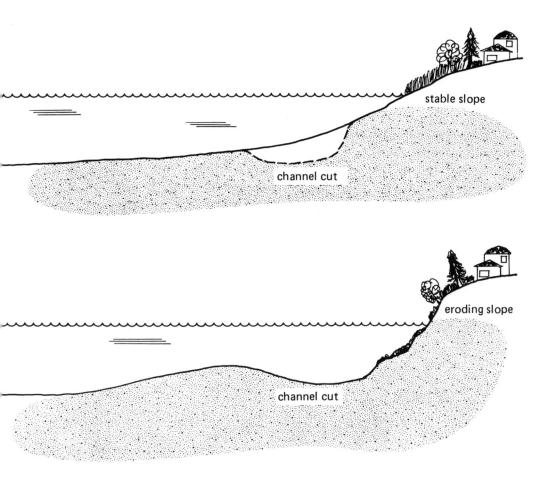

Figure 77. Improperly located navigation channels result in shore erosion.

unaltered (page 73). Major aspects of landfilling for housing and dredging of access canals are discussed under Residential Development (page 161). Ditching of wetlands is discussed in Mosquito Control (page 145). Major ecological disturbances are caused by various inland canals and ditches through alteration of the natural hydrologic patterns essential to the well-being of coastal ecosystems.

Canal dredging projects are so diverse that it is difficult to suggest specific constraints. Generally, alternative solutions should be found that eliminate the need for canals. Those that are essential to the public, and for which there are not alternate solutions, are to be minimized in extent, designed with care, and built under stringent environmental controls.

The Federal Refuse Act (33 U.S.C. 403–1899) assigns primary regulatory and permitting authority for dredge and fill activities in *navigable waters* to the U.S. Army Corps of Engineers. The permit process provides for the issuance of a public notice and for public comments on economics, navigation, conservation, aesthetics, historic value, fish and wildlife values, flood damage prevention, recreation, land use, water supply, water quality, general environmental concerns and in general the needs and welfare of the people. In addition to its regulatory responsibility the Corps of Engineers dredges enormous volumes of material annually in the construction and continual maintenance of navigable waterways, harbors and ports; the Intracoastal Waterway; flood protection projects; and for beach restoration and enhancement. The Corps of Engineers spends over $100 million yearly just to maintain U.S. navigable waterways.[112]

The Fish and Wildlife Coordination Act (1956) requires that the Corps of Engineers consult with the Bureau of Sport Fisheries and Wildlife (Interior) and the National Marine Fisheries Service (Commerce) with regard to potential effects of any dredge and fill activities on fish and wildlife resources. The U.S. Environmental Protection Agency is also involved through the Ocean Dumping Act (1972) and the Federal Water Pollution Control Act (1970) and amendments (1972). In addition to Federal requirements for dredge and fill, a variety of state agencies may exercise some degree of control or permitting authority.

Recommended Constraints:

1. Coastal navigation channels are to be located away from vital areas and far enough from the shoreline so as not to unstabilize and erode the shore.

2. Navigation channel depth and width are to be designed to the absolute minimum size required.

3. The sides of dredged channels are to be cut initially to the full expected equilibrium slope.

4. Overboard disposal of polluted or soft dredge spoils is unacceptable.

5. Polluted or soft dredge spoils are to be disposed of in safe upland areas or deep ocean sites.

6. With proper ecological safeguards certain dredge spoils can be used to build marshland or islands.

7. Wetlands and tidelands are not to be filled, drained by ditching, canalized for access, or pre-empted or altered for other purposes, except when there is no alternative to serve public needs.

EXTRACTIVE INDUSTRIES

Oil, gas, sand, gravel, shells, salt, phosphate and hard minerals are among the resources extracted from estuaries and open coastal waters through a variety of techniques. Each specific extractive process has a certain potential for disturbance of coastal land/water ecosystems. This potential is to be carefully compared with public benefits before permission is granted.

Construction industries use enormous amounts of sand and gravel. About 90 percent of the sand and gravel sold in the United States is used for making concrete. As construction needs force the demand for sand and gravel higher each year, and as sand and gravel pits on land near urban areas become depleted, coastal deposits become more tempting, particularly those available at the bottoms of estuaries. Powerful hydraulic dredges make estuarine mining practicable and profitable. Sand can be dredged for less than $1.00 per yard and sold for $2.00 to $3.00 per yard—costs of transportation from dredge to construction site govern profit. About 10 percent of commercial sand and gravel comes from submerged coastal beds—about 100 million tons per year, worth perhaps $250 million on-site.[123]

The same sort of potential for ecologic disruption exists for sand and gravel mining as for any dredging operation—turbidity, sedimentation, loss of productive bottom, a diminishing of plant life, shellfish beds, fish stocks and so forth (page 101). In addition, circulation characteristics are altered as channels are widened or deepened with pronounced environmental effects (page 42). Where excavation leaves depressions in the estuarine bottom, foul conditions result from reduction of oxygen (page 103).

Elimination of most sand and gravel dredging from estuaries is required along with careful control of offshore dredging. There should be exceptions in places where sand is continuously deposited by water currents and therefore is a *renewable* resource. Controls must be enforced based on an environmentally sound plan. The mining may be done in conjunction with channel dredging so long as the need is real and not just a profit gimmick disguised as a bonafide navigation improvement project.

A promising alternative to mining in ecologically sensitive estuaries is to dredge sand and gravel offshore on the Continental Shelf.[113] New methods and equipment required for offshore mining are under development. Ecological hazards do exist and offshore mining will have to be controlled. Also, dredging too close to shore causes sandy beaches and dunes to slump away into the ocean (page 150). Under no circumstances should dredging be done landward of the open surf zone (30-40 feet depth).

Strip mining of shell beds poses serious ecological threats to estuaries. Large deposits of oyster shell in shallow bottoms from North Carolina to Texas, and in San Francisco Bay, are useful for making cement, poultry grit, soil conditioners and other calcium based products. Clam shell is sometimes dredged for roadway surfaces, but is too dense for conversion to calcium products.[78]

Turbidity in the area of shell dredging may be ten times higher than that caused by current, wind or boat traffic. Shell dredging also leads to "density" mud flows that cover and suffocate the life in their path (at sediment concentrations of 100-175 gr. per liter). These mud flows may extend 1,500 to 2,000 feet from the dredge.[114] Other potential effects from shell dredging include: serious reduction of dissolved oxygen in the area,[114] eutrophication and alteration of current flows by change of basin shape.

To prevent gross pollution it is often recommended that dredges remain 1,200 feet away from live oyster reefs and other *vital areas*.[78] But in Mobile Bay, Alabama—where 20 miles of trench are dredged and 2 million cubic yards of shell removed per year—currents from winds of 12-15 m.p.h. create a turbidity plume visible for 1.5 miles behind the dredge. NASA aerial photographs showed a plume 20 miles long and half a mile wide at slightly higher winds.[114] Clearly a 1,200 foot buffer would not be adequate protection under these conditions.

Shell dredging is a dubious enterprise with little public value and a high potential for public detriment. Calcium can be supplied from elsewhere.

Fresh water supplies are extracted from seawater for municipal use in certain coastal areas. Desalination is an expensive process and generally only feasible in island areas. In 1967, there were 286 freshwater conversion plants in the country.[78] The major disturbances are thermal pollution (page 134), and high salinity discharge.

Table salt is produced by evaporation of seawater. In San Francisco Bay, thousands of acres of marshland have been unwisely pre-empted for evaporation ponds and removed from the estuarine ecosystem. Magnesium compounds, gypsum, bromine, and bittern (containing many elements) are side products.[115]

Extraction of hard minerals from bedrock and placer deposits is not now significant. However, there is a potential for gold, titanium, zerconium, tin, chromium, copper, zinc and nickel by various mining techniques. For example, a copper-zinc mine is operating in Penobscot Bay, Maine; a titanium recovery operation is in the marshland area of Tom's River, New Jersey; and a barite mine is at Castle Island, Alaska.[116] Such operations can create numerous pollution problems and disturbances.

Phosphate strip mining for fertilizer poses a special ecologic problem.

For example, in a 9,000 acre tract on the Pamlico Estuary (N.C.), leased from the state, cofferdams and pumps are used to expose the phosphate deposits on the estuary bottom. The hazards are turbidity, sedimentation and particularly eutrophication which results when there is sufficient nitrogen in the water to combine with the excess phosphate released by the constant pumping of water from behind the cofferdam.[12] Coastal deposits of phosphorous should not be mined because of the high potential for ecologic damage. Georgia rejected a bid for phosphate mining because it would obliterate marshland.[116]

Oil and gas extraction, transport and refining have the potential for serious adverse effects on coastal ecosystems. Major disturbances are: (1) general disruption of the marine environment from dredging, barge traffic and so forth (page 101), (2) pre-emption or degradation of environmental *vital areas* (e.g., wetlands) and (3) pollution by oil spills from blowouts, pipeline ruptures and ship collision and other transport accidents, which can seriously damage water quality, waterfowl, fish and coastal ecosystems.[118, 125]

Other sources contributing to coastal ecosystem degradation are vessel de-ballasting and bilge pumping, detergent and chemical clean-up techniques and general oil transfer operations including pipeline leakage. Nearshore and estuarine areas are vulnerable to offshore spills through wind, ocean current and tidal transport of oil shoreward. Efforts to clean up these pollutants with chemical techniques may also be detrimental to coastal plants and animals by placing additional stresses on the ecosystem.

The major deleterious effects of petroleum pollution are: (1) disruption of physiological and behavioral patterns of feeding and reproductive activities; (2) direct mortality from toxic ingredients; (3) changes in physical and chemical habitat, causing exclusion of species and reduction of populations; and (4) serious energy demands on the ecosystem from decomposition of refinery effluents resulting in altered productivity, metabolism, system structure and species diversity (Figure 78).

All phases of production—extraction, transport and refining—have the potential for serious environmental impacts on coastal waters. Extraction in wetland areas and near-coastal waters is the most dangerous in terms of the risk to coastal ecosystems. Pipeline ruptures in wetlands could permanently damage a valuable coastal resource. Over 100,000 metric tons of oil pollution results each year from such ruptures.[117]

Although offshore extraction technology is improving rapidly, environmental protection technology is lagging far behind.[25] In a recent assessment, three areas of inadequacy in safety devices were found: "velocity-actuated down-hole safety devices, well control technologies, and oil

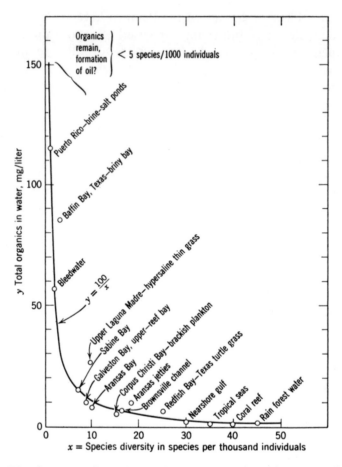

Figure 78. Species diversity and total organic substances in water, including oil.[124]

containment and clean-up devices."[119] Petroleum discharge from spills, seeps, blowouts, pipeline ruptures, etc., is acutely toxic to virtually all marine and coastal organisms.[125] Immobile or passive forms such as aquatic plants, many shellfish and plankton may be especially susceptible because they cannot escape.

Pipeline construction requires dredging, often including wide barge canals for the laying of equipment. These canals, dredged to 40 or more feet in width, traverse and cut through marshlands and estuaries affecting natural drainage patterns, disrupting currents in bays and waterflow in marshlands, and reducing animal and plant populations from dredging, turbidity and sedimentation within the rights-of-way (page 101).

Extraction from offshore areas of the Continental Shelf poses specific threats to coastal ecosystems by way of facilities for transfer, refining, storage and reshipment of petroleum products and crew and construction centers. Any facilities proposal should be rejected that would preempt *vital areas,* pose a significant pollution threat, disrupt drainage water flows, reduce natural productivity or otherwise degrade coastal ecosystems. Consequently, assessment of offshore oil activities is to include a searching review of impacts from onshore facilities. Much of the coastline is clearly unsuitable for onshore facilities. A smaller fraction will be capable of supporting some development with rigid environmental safeguards.

Onshore facilities involve construction of:

1. Tranmission pipelines and onshore pumping stations.

2. Channels, docks, buildings and roadways to accommodate water and land traffic at transfer facilities.

3. Onshore crew facilities and construction bases.

4. Refineries and associated petrochemical industries at or near onshore receiving stations.

5. Induced secondary development; supporting commercial and industrial facilities.

6. Residential development and community support for people working in and living near these facilities (population about seven times that of facility employment).

Recommended Constraints:

1. No sand or gravel is to be removed from estuaries except in areas where active shoaling is taking place and then only the accreting amounts, provided the shoal is not a *vital area.*

2. Mining shall be controlled following the same guidelines as for any dredging.

3. Offshore mining may be conducted only outside the active surf zone (depths greater than 30-40 feet), and away from *vital areas.*

4. Shell dredging is to be phased out in favor of other sources of lime.

5. Preemption of wetlands by the creation of salt ponds or dredging and strip mining for phosphate or other minerals should be discouraged.

6. Strip mining is to be prohibited in the coastal zone in favor of upland and offshore sources.

7. Oil drilling is to be restricted from areas where petroleum would be leaked or spilled into *vital areas* or

carried there by currents or winds.

8. Shoreside facilities for oil drilling or other extractive operations are to follow all general development constraints set forth for heavy industry and other relevant activities.

HEAVY INDUSTRY

Heavy industry in coastal areas produces several types of adverse environmental impacts including: pre-emption of coastal *vital areas;* impacts of extensive secondary development induced by the presence of the industry; and the generation of pollutants and wastewater.

Many industries are waterfront located of necessity (e.g., shipping terminals and seafood processing plants). But most are there because of low cost of coastal lowlands or the access to markets and supplies via water transportation and they do not require waterfront location. Coastal wetland and tideland pre-empted for industry sites reduces the productivity and quality of estuarine and coastal ecosystems (page 68). The pollutants generated endanger coastal organisms and water quality. As a general rule, industrial activities not requiring coastal location, *sine qua non,* should not be located in the coastal zone (floodplain to water's edge).

The predictable impact of an industrial area includes the secondary development induced by the presence of the industry. For example, a factory may attract new housing project, shopping centers and other ancillary development on surrounding lands. The demands placed upon a community's environmental protection facilities by both the factory and its induced development will be far greater than those of the factory itself. For example, one may estimate an induced population at least seven times the industry employment base. Therefore, any decision on a proposed industrial site must include full consideration of the secondary development it will induce.

Other than the land use aspects, well covered elsewhere in this guidebook, specific industry problems relate to the pollutants and wastewater that they generate. These vary widely in nature and volume. Figure 79 presents a general characterization of the wastewater generated by 18 major types of industry. For each type, 23 wastewater characteristics are analyzed in terms of their potential impact upon coastal ecosystems. The impacts range from relatively minor disruptions (such as temporary, localized turbidity increase) to biotic destruction (discharge of toxic chemicals).

The Federal Water Act Amendments of 1972 have as a goal the elimination of all discharge of polluting substances to U.S. waters by 1985.[29]

158

POTENTIAL ECOLOGICAL IMPACT OF INDUSTRIAL WASTEWATER, BY INDUSTRIAL TYPE (SOURCE: U.S. ENVIRONMENTAL PROTECTION AGENCY).

INDUSTRIAL ACTIVITY	SUSPENDED SOLIDS	DISSOLVED SOLIDS	NITROGEN	PHOSPHORUS	TURBIDITY	TEMPERATURE	DISSOLVED GASSES	COLLOIDAL SOLIDS	pH	COLOR	HEAVY METALS	CYANIDE	VOLATILE ORGANICS	DETERGENTS	FOAMING	PESTICIDES	PHENOL	SULFIDES	OIL AND GREASE	BOD	COD	COLIFORM (FECAL)	COLIFORM (TOTAL)
PAPER AND ALLIED PRODUCTS	○	○	●	●	●	●	○	○	○	○	○				○				●	○	●		
GRAIN MILLING AND DAIRY PRODUCTS	○	○	○	○	○	○		○	○	○				○	○				○	○	○	○	●
TEXTILES	○	●	●	○	○	○		○	○	●	●			○	○				○	○	○	○	NA
SEAFOODS AND MEAT PRODUCTS	○	○	○	○	○	○		●		○				○			●		●	○	○	●	NA
PHARMACEUTICALS	●	○	○	○	○	○		●	○	○	○	○	●	○	○				○	○	○		○
LEATHER TANNING AND FINISHING	●	●		●	○			○	○	○	○	○		○	○			●	●	●	●		○
SUGAR, BEVERAGES, FRUITS/VEGETABLES	○	○	●	●	○	○	○		○	○			○		○	○	○			○	○		○
PETROLEUM REFINING		○		●		●	○		○		●	●	○						●	●	●		○
PLASTIC/SYNTHETIC MATERIALS	○	○	○	●	○	○		○	○		○		○	○			○		○	○	○		
BLAST FURNACES, STEEL WORKS [1]	○	○	○	●	○	●	○	○	○		○	○	○	○			○	○	○				
ORGANIC CHEMICALS	○	○	○	●		○	○		○		●	○	○	○	○		○	○	○	○	○	○	○
METAL FINISHING	○	●	○	○	○			○	○		●	○	○						●				
INORGANIC FERTILIZERS		●		○	NA	○	○		○	NA				NA		NA	NA	NA	○				
ELECTRIC AND STEAM POWER GENERATION	○	●	●	●		●		○		●	●	○	○	○					●		●		
ALUMINUM	●		●	○	○	○	○		○	○		○			○				●				
FLAT GLASS, CEMENT, LIME [2]		○	●	○	○	○		○	○	○				○									
INORGANIC CHEMICALS		○	●	●	NA	○		NA	○	NA	○	○			NA		NA	NA				NA	NA
INDUSTRIAL GAS PRODUCTS			●	●		○			○						NA				●				

● = SEVERE
○ = VARIABLE
 = SLIGHT
NA = DATA NOT AVAILABLE

[1] ALSO "ROLLING AND FINISHING"
[2] ALSO "CONCRETE PRODUCTS, GYPSUM AND ASBESTOS"

Figure 79. Potential for ecosystem disturbance associated with various industrial activity types.

Federal and state requirements under the law should correct pollution problems, as explained below:[120]

The effects of all of these forms of pollution can be eliminated by the application of existing waste treatment technology and recognition of the characteristics of the estuarine environment which is the final disposal point of the treated waste discharge. Even estuaries which are heavily polluted now can be reclaimed if the wastes entering them are adequately treated.

Recommended Constraints:

1. Industries not wholly dependent upon waterfront location are to be placed inland.
2. Industries are not to be located so as to preempt or endanger *vital areas*.
3. Assessments of the impact of a proposed site are to include the secondary development induced by the industry.
4. Pollution control standards are to be strictly enforced.
5. All general land and water use constraints previously set forth are to be followed.

COMMUNITY SOLID WASTE DISPOSAL

There are special ecological problems concerned with community solid wastes—garbage and trash—in coastal areas. Most of these can be solved by locating disposal areas away from ecologically sensitive shore areas and by the proper design and operation of disposal sites.

It is unacceptable to pre-empt *vital areas*—wetlands, tidelands, drainageways—for disposal sites for two major reasons: (1) such areas are essential ecosystem components and (2) wastes deposited in tidally flushed areas have a high potential for gross pollution of coastal waters. It is equally unacceptable to dump community wastes directly into estuarine or ocean waters. Nor are coastal floodplain (*areas of environmental concern*) sites normally acceptable because of probable pollution from nutrient and chemicals toxic to aquatic life that are carried into coastal waters by: (1) storm flooding and (2) precipitation and land drainage. Even well designed sanitary landfills are a potential source of coastal water pollution when located in coastal floodplains.

The continuous leaching of one acre-foot of landfill may be expected to yield the following amounts of pollutants which increase BOD, eutrophication and turbidity each year:[121]

| Sodium | 1.5 tons | Chloride | 0.9 tons |
| Potassium | 1.5 tons | Sulfate | 0.2 tons |

160

Calcium	1.0 ton	Bicarbonate	3.9 tons
Magnesium	1.0 ton		

Ecologic hazards of disposal in shorelands stem from contamination or disruption of flow patterns of water that drains from the coastal watershed into estuarine water basins (page 42). The following standard water quality precautions are necessary to protect coastal ecosystems:

  1. Locate landfills far enough away from watercourses to avoid water pollution.

  2. Locate land fills so as to avoid significant disruption of normal drainage patterns in the water-proofing of sites.

The following procedures are useful in reducing the total volume of wastes and consequently the extent of landfill: (1) mechanical compaction of wastes, (2) incineration with control of air pollutants, (3) hauling to inland sites ($5 per ton, less than 50 miles),[122] (4) reuse of economically recoverable wastes and (5) reduction of sources of waste.

Recommended Constraints:

  1. Solid waste disposal sites are to be located out of coastal floodplains, wetlands, tidelands and water areas.

  2. In coastal watersheds, locate solid disposal sites away from waterdrainage courses, well above the high ground water level, and so as not to interfere with normal drainage flow patterns.

RESIDENTIAL DEVELOPMENT

The process of residential development in coastal areas involves a complex of potential ecologic disturbances to coastal waters, both from construction activity and from human occupancy and activity. The degree of disturbance is heightened by: (1) increased density of development, (2) closer proximity to the water, (3) extensive alteration of the shorescape and (4) the ecologic sensitivity of the ecosystem. In general, constraints appropriate to residential development depend upon the elevation of the land to be developed.

The assessment of environmental impacts of residential development in coastal areas must include the full effect of all ancillary development. A coastal residential community requires roads, marinas, storm drain systems, parking lots, waste treatment facilities and so forth. Each of these has the potential for disturbance of coastal ecosystems.

There is no important difference between "primary home" and "second home" developments other than those accounted for by characteristics of design and location of the community and individual homes.

The major sources of disturbance of the coastal ecosystem are: (1)

pollution of coastal waters, (2) interference with water flows in the watershed or in the coastal water basin and (3) preemption or degradation of *vital areas*.

Residential construction pollutes coastal waters largely through the erosion that results from land clearing (page 40) and site preparation (page 125). These activities cause discharge into coastal waters ("nonpoint" pollution) of sediment (page 125) and nutrients (page 38). Residential occupancy pollutes coastal waters through sewage discharge (page 121) and contamination of land drainage (urban runoff) by sediment, nutrient and toxic substances (page 140).

Shoreland or shoreline residential development alters waterflows leading to ecosystem disturbance mainly by: (1) blocking shoreland drainageways or regrading the land surface (page 125), (2) creating impervious surfaces (page 38) and installation of storm drain systems (page 141), (3) shortcircuiting natural drainage flows with access canals (page 42), (4) causing salt water intrusion of ground water by canals (page 38) and (5) increasing tidal prism by canal excavation and navigation channel deepening in the adjoining water basin (page 42). Canals collect pollutants, become foul and contaminate estuarine waters (page 101). Serious and often irreversible pollution also may result from sediments dispersed in channel dredging operations (Figure 80).

Further ecosystem disturbance may result from bulkheading and other attempts to prevent erosion of occupied shorelines (page 96). Incidental problems of coastal area occupancy arise from natural storm and flood hazards (page 96), unsuitable soils for foundations or drainage, and shortage of fresh water supplies.

The shorelands above the coastal floodplain are *areas of normal concern* and require only the precautions typical of thoughtful planning of residential development. Insofar as the coastal waters are concerned, preservation of the natural patterns of drainage water flow (page 42) and prevention of runoff water contamination are important.

The coastal floodplains are *areas of environmental concern,* have limited carrying capacity and require appropriate development precautions. Special efforts will be needed to preserve drainage because these areas have a high water table and a direct hydraulic connection to coastal waters (page 95). Also their proximity to the shore means that polluted runoff goes quickly to the coastal water basin with little time for natural purification through vegetation and soil. Therefore, development will be at lower densities, buffer areas will be required (page 42) and special attention will be given to land grading and drainage.[66]

The estuarine shoreline corridor often contains *vital areas* which are an

162

Figure 80. Dredging in estuarine areas has a high potential for ecosystem disturbance (Michael Fahey, Sandy Hook Marine Laboratory).

irreplaceable and essential component of the ecosystem they serve (page 59), and therefore are to be left undeveloped and are to receive full protection from degrading influences. *Vital areas* that are not to be pre-empted by conversion to residential use include drainageways, wetlands, vegetated tidelands, productive tideflats and sand dunes.

Waterfront development by dredging wetlands, tidelands and estuarine bottoms and using the "spoil" to fill and elevate the land is the most disturbing of all types of residential development and should be discontinued. Residences can be located above the wetlands and water access can be provided at community facilities.

Recommended Constraints:

    1. In shorelands above the coastal floodplain, normal precautions are required to prevent interference with the

natural pattern of drainage and to prevent contamination of runoff water.

2. In the coastal floodplain, special precautions are required to protect drainage flows and to prevent pollution of coastal waters through contaminated runoff; development density will be at a lower level than in upland areas.

3. *Vital areas* such as wetlands, tidelands, sand dunes and drainageways are not to be converted to residential use.

4. All constraints on development previously set forth are to be respected, as appropriate, in the planning, location, construction and occupancy of coastal communities.

APPENDIX

FEDERAL COASTAL ZONE MANAGEMENT PROGRAM

The U.S. Coastal Zone Management Act of 1972 (P.L. 92-583) provides, *among other things*, a plan of support and guidance for state and local management of coastal land and water use. The Federal program has two phases: (1) planning and (2) management. To qualify for the management phase, a state must first meet the requirements of the planning phase (Sect. 305). Guidelines and criteria for the planning phase are described in "Coastal Zone Management Program Development Grants" (Federal Register, 38(113), Pt. III, pg. 15538). A number of these guidelines and criteria contain references to matters that require ecologic interpretation. We review below material presented in this handbook that provides background information on these matters along with some suggested interpretations.

COASTAL WATERS

In the Act, coastal waters are defined, in part, as "those waters adjacent to the shorelines which contain a measurable quantity or percentage of seawater" and which extend seaward to the outer limit of United States jurisdiction. This is useful principally in establishing a boundary across open waters of tidal rivers—where fresh meets salt water—and not for establishing a boundary along the shore where salt water meets the land.

"Measurable quantity or percentage of seawater" has no official or generally accepted definition. The critical question is where one draws the line between ocean and fresh water in various tidal rivers. The boundary between measurable amounts of seawater and non-measurable amounts would occur in the vicinity of the "salt front," the arbitrary interface between seawater and undiluted fresh water. Here the vagaries of tide, runoff and wind are such that the front is in constant movement and may vary up and down a large tidal river basin as many as 20 miles or more. At any fixed point, abutting this shifting front, the salinity may vary as much as 10 parts per thousand (ppt) or more, from time to time.

For practical purposes of defining coastal waters, we recommend that a value of 0.5 ppt be used as the least "measurable quantity or percentage of seawater" because it can be detected by simple field equipment and because it is the lowest value that consistently could be ascribed an important ecologic meaning in most cases.

In view of the larger problems of defining boundaries in this area of oscillating salinity, it would seem unreasonable to require the high level of accuracy that is available only with sophisticated laboratory equipment.

Because the 0.5 ppt salt front shifts up and down the estuary basin under the influence of wind, tide and runoff, it is difficult to choose a fixed boundary for the inner edge of coastal waters. We expect that for practical reasons a fixed permanent boundary would be required for management in most cases, rather than a boundary that shifts with the position of the salt front. In choosing such a fixed management boundary we recommend that it be set at the point of maximum probable penetration of a "measurable quantity of seawater" (0.5 ppt) during the course of an average year. For practical purposes, and to avoid the complications of extraordinary events, the boundary might be set at that point above which the "measurable quantity of seawater" is found in the bottom waters less than one percent of the time during an average year's hydrologic cycle (or some other percentage that would fit the particular case).

Another satisfactory method for fixing the inner boundary of measurable salt is a biotic survey. The fixed (immobile) biotic community of tidal rivers and similar areas varies with the salt content of the water. The proportion of various species gradually shifts from the sea toward the head of the estuary. At the point where the salt content falls below an average of about 0.5 ppt there is a sudden and dramatic change which signals the ecological boundary between the estuary and fresh waters, or the ecological point above which there is no longer a "measurable amount" of salt. This boundary would be useful in setting the inner boundary of coastal waters because it integrates the effects of the whole range of variation in salinity on a long term basis. Specifically, the boundary should be drawn at the point where the fixed biotic community shifts to over 50 percent endemic fresh water forms of life in any category (molluscs, gastropods, nematodes, etc.). A more expanded management area may be needed to include the *fresh water* spawning areas of anadromous tidal fishes such as striped bass, salmon, and shad.

A similar biotic survey can be made in the shorelands to determine the inner extent of salt water influence. A botanist can study the flora and determine the line above which there is no "measurable" effect of salt water inundation or penetration. In shorelands, each species of plant

166

has a degree of tolerance to salt in the water that surrounds it or surrounds its roots in the earth. Because of the different degrees of tolerance of various plants, there is a gradation in plant species from the water body up the shoreland slope. It is relatively easy for a botanist to find the point above which there is no significant growth of salt water tolerant plants. This would be the inner boundary of coastal waters in the shorelands and might approximate the point of the highest expected yearly storm surge (the highest level to be expected from normal storms during the course of a year).

SHORELANDS

We use "shorelands" to mean the terrain of the coastal watershed down to the upper margin of the wetlands (lower margin of floodplain). A coastal watershed is a drainage basin immediately adjacent to coastal waters which is comprised of lands, all or some of which drain directly into coastal waters, and *does not* include lands of drainage basins that drain wholly into fresh water channels tributary to coastal waters.

These shorelands all have *potential* "direct and significant impact on the coastal waters" as stated in the Federal Act, and must be included in the management program in order to protect coastal waters from pollution by sediment, nutrient and toxic pollutants and to stabilize the volume and periodicity of the flow of fresh water into coastal water basins. There should be an initial *presumption* of significant impact of all development in shorelands and, therefore, they should all be encompassed within the boundaries of the coastal zone management district. Subsequently it may be discovered that much of the shoreland area is not situated so as to cause significant disturbances of coastal waters, because of topographic or drainage details. Such shorelands should require no special constraints for the protection of coastal waters (these lands would be in an "area of normal concern," or "Utilization" Class). However, it should be anticipated that in the floodplain all lands will probably require special restrictions ("Areas of Environmental Concern" or "Conservation" Class). The wetlands and the tidelands are part of the coastal waters regime and are designated for complete protection ("Vital Areas" or "Preservation" Class).

AREAS OF PARTICULAR CONCERN

The Guidelines of the Federal Act list the following representative factors as those to be taken into account when designating "Areas of Particular Concern" as required by the Act:

1. Areas of unique, scarce, fragile or vulnerable natural

habitat, physical feature, historical significance, cultural value and scenic importance;

2. Areas of high natural productivity or essential habitat for living resources, including fish, wildlife and the various trophic levels in the food web critical to their well-being;

3. Areas of substantial recreational value and/or opportunity;

4. Areas where developments and facilities are dependent upon the utilization of, or access to, coastal waters;

5. Areas of unique geologic or topographic significance to industrial or commercial development;

6. Areas of urban concentration where shoreline utilization and water uses are highly competitive; and

7. Areas of significant hazard if developed, due to storms, slides, floods, erosion, settlement, etc.

Areas designated for "particular concern" with the object of conserving coastal resources are scheduled to be preserved or restored for conservation, recreation, ecologic, or aesthetic purposes. Such areas appear to be equivalent either to our *areas of environmental concern* or to our *vital areas*. There does not appear to be any intended differentiation of areas that are "vital" and areas that are of "concern" in the Federal program. This differentiation, it seems, might be useful in allowing more specificity of goals and more flexibility in management. Therefore, we suggest that areas of "particular concern" be understood to mean a larger general area of concern, or *areas of environmental concern,* and that *vital areas* be used for those exceptionally valuable ecologic areas within them.

GLOSSARY

Brief definitions are given below for many technical terms or words which we have used with special meaning. More detailed definitions of the terms can be found in various technical glossaries.

Adverse effects. An adverse reaction of an ecosystem to a *disturbance.*

Agitation dredging. A method of dredging that involves overboard discharge of spoil with a high induced rate of dispersal.

Anadromous. Oceanic or estuarine species that spawn in fresh water.

Areas of environmental concern. Areas which, because of their environmental significance, require special management considerations.

Barrier island. Elongate seafront islands formed by the action of the sea.

Bay. A large estuary with a relatively high degree of flushing.

Benthos. The community of bottom-dwelling life.

Berm. A formation of sand deposited just above normal high water by wave action.

Biochemical oxygen demand. A measure of the amount of oxygen required to oxidize compounds by biochemical processes.

Biocide. Manufactured poison.

Biomass. The mass of living matter in a given space.

Biota. The plant and animal assemblage of a biologic community.

Brackish. Fresh water mixed with a small proportion of salt water.

Buffer area. A limited use area between a developed area and a protected area.

Carrying capacity. (Ecology) The limit to the amount of life, in numbers or mass, that can be supported by any given habitat. (In another context, used to express reasonable limits of human use of a resource.

Circulation. The pattern of movement of water in a coastal basin.

Climax state. The final equilibrium community reached in the process of *succession.*

Closed cycle. A self-contained power plant steam-condenser cooling system that requires water input only to replace evaporative losses and to dilute residues.

Coastal. Of or pertaining to the seacoast (or Great Lakes shore); specifically *shorelands,* estuarine basins, and the nearshore ocean.

Coastal upwelling. A process by which water moves shoreward along the bottom of a water basin into the shore zone; reaction caused usually by wind forcing surface waters offshore.

Coastal waters. Waters adjacent to the shoreline which contain a measurable quantity or percentage of sea water.

Coastal watershed. A drainage basin that drains directly into coastal waters. (Does not include drainage basins that drain wholly into fresh water channels tributary to coastal waters.)

Confinement. The degree of closure of a coastal water basin.

Consumers. Plant eaters.

Cut. See *gut.*

Decomposers. Microorganisms that decompose tissue.

Detritus. Particles of plant matter in varying stages of decomposition.

Disturbance. A disruption, or perturbation, of an ecosystem resulting from human activity.

Diversity. The variety of species present in a biological *community.*

Diversity index. A measure of *diversity.*

Drainageway. A pathway for watershed drainage characterized by wet soil vegetation; often intermittent in flow.

Drainage basin. The entire area of shorelands drained by a watercourse in such a way that all flow originating in the area is discharged through a single outlet.

Ecology. The science which relates living forms to their environment.

Ecologic effect. The reaction of an ecosystem to an ecologic disturbance.

Ecotone. The transition area at the border of two different biological communities.

Eddy. A water current moving contrary to the direction of the main current, especially in a circular motion.

Embayment. A relatively small and shallow estuary with rather restricted flushing (differs from lagoon by having significant freshwater inflow).

Endemic. A species of limited geographic extent.

Entrainment. Removal of suspended life from an aquatic ecosystem by withdrawal of water.

Environmental impact. An environmental change that affects human needs (c.f. *ecologic effect*).

Estuary. Any confined coastal water body with an open connection to the sea and a measurable quantity of salt in its waters. ("Confined" means shoreline length greater and 3 times width of opening. "Measurable" means greater than 0.5 ppt).

Eutrophication. Nutrient enrichment, leading to excessive growth of aquatic plants.

Evapotranspiration. A collective term for the processes of evaporation and plant transpiration by which water is returned to the atmosphere.

Fauna. A collective term for the animal species present in an ecosystem.

Filling. Artificial elevation of land by deposit of soil or sediment.

Flocculation. The process by which very fine particles in suspension collect into larger masses, which eventually settle out of the water column.

Floodplain. The area of shorelands extending inland from the normal yearly maximum storm water level to the highest expected storm water level in a given period of time (i.e., 5, 50, 100 years).

Flora. A collective term for the plant species present in an ecosystem.

Flushing rate. The rate at which the water of an estuary is replaced (usually expressed as the time for one complete replacement).

Food chain. The step-by-step transfer of food energy and materials, by consumption, from the primary source in plants through to increasingly higher forms of fauna.

Food web. The network of feeding relationships in a biological community.

Foragers. Animals that feed on *consumers.*

Gut. A narrow, deep channel that is usually characterized by rapid currents.

Habitat. The place of residence of an animal species or a community of species.

Impact assessment. The evaluation of ecological effects to determine their impact on human needs.

Indicator species. A species chosen to represent some particular environmental condition.

Intertidal areas. The area between high and low tide levels.

Lagoon. A relatively shallow estuary with very restricted exchange with the sea and no significant fresh water inflow.

Longshore current. A current running parallel and adjacent to the shoreline.

Nursery area. A place where young stages of aquatic life concentrate for feeding or refuge.

Pathogenic. Capable of causing disease.

Performance standard. A specific measure for control of a human activity.

Photosynthesis. The manufacture of carbohydrate food from carbon dioxide and water in the presence of chlorophyll, by utilizing light energy, and releasing oxygen.

Phytoplankton. The plant component of the plankton.

Plankton. Small suspended aquatic plants or animals which passively drift or swim weakly.

Predators. Animals that feed primarily on *foragers.*

Primary productivity. The amount of organic matter produced by photosynthesis.

Producers. Green plants, photosynthesizers.

Pump-storage plant. A hydro-electric generating facility operated by the flow of artificially elevated water.

Rookery. A communal breeding site of certain shore birds and seals.

Salinity. A measure of the quantity of dissolved salts in sea water (in parts per thousand of water:ppt).

Salt front. The inland limit of measurable salt (0.5 ppt) in an estuary at any given time.

Salt water intrusion. A movement of salt water inland into fresh water aquifers.

Sedimentation. The process of gravitational deposition of soil and other particles transported by water.

Shoaling. Reduction of depth of a water basin.

Shorelands. The terrain of the coastal watershed down to the upper margin of the wetlands (lower margin of coastal floodplain).

Sidecast disposal. The simplest technique for overboard disposal whereby *spoil* is discharged directly to the water.

Silt. Fine particulate matter suspended in water.

Slough. See *swale.*

Spoil. Dredged materials.

Standing crop. The number (or mass) of a species (or all species) in a specified area at a given time.

Storage. Capability of a biological system to store energy supplies in one or more of its components.

Stratified estuary. An estuary with two distinct water layers flowing in opposite directions.

Succession. A systematic series of species replacements in a biological system.

Surfacing. Installation of impervious material over the land.

Swale. A low-lying area commonly moist or marshy; an intermittent drainageway.

Tidal river. The tidally influenced portion of a coastal river.

Tide flat. An unvegetated intertidal area.

Tide levels. See Figure 55 in text.

Tide rip. A shearing of two adjacent currents causing a noticeable surface discontinuity.

Tideland. The intertidal area.

Toxic substance. A poison.

Trophic level. A step in the *food chain.*

Turbidity. Reduced water clarity resulting from presence of suspended matter.

Vegetated tidelands. A vegetated *intertidal* area.

Vital area. A physical component, or feature, of such extreme importance to the functioning of an ecosystem that it requires complete preservation.

Wetlands. Naturally vegetated areas located between mean high water and the yearly normal maximum flood water level.

Zooplankton. The animal component of the plankton.

NOTES

1. Odum, E. P. 1971. *Fundamentals of ecology.* W. B. Saunders Co. Philadelphia.
2. Pritchard, D. W. 1967. What is an estuary? physical viewpoint. In *Estuaries* (G. E. Lauff, ed.). Am. Assn. Adv. Sci., Publ. No. 83:3-5.
3. U.S. Dept. of Interior. 1970. *The national estuarine pollution study.* U.S. Senate, 91st Congress, 2nd Session. Document No. 91-58.
4. Postma, H. 1967. Sediment transport and sedimentation in the estuarine environment. In *Estuaries* (G. E. Lauff, ed.). Am. Assn. Adv. Sci., Publ. No. 83:158-180.
5. National Science Foundation. 1973. Managing coastal lands. *Mosaic.* Vol. 4, No. 3:26-32. (from Coast. Res. Mgt. Prog., Div. of Plan. Coord., State of Texas).
6. City of Bellevue. 1971. Environmental focus. A City of Bellevue planning study. Planning Dept., Bellevue, Wash.
7. Governor's Task Force. 1972. *The coastal zone of Delaware.* College of Marine Studies. Univ. of Delaware. Newark, Del.
8. Jaworski, N. A., D. W. Lear, Jr., and O. Villa, Jr. 1972. Nutrient management in the Potomac Estuary. In *Nutrients and eutrophication: the limiting nutrient controversy.* (G. E. Likens, ed.). Limn. and Ocean. Soc. Spec. Symp. Vol. I:259-263.
9. Kraijenhoff van de Leur, D. A. 1972. Rainfall-runoff relations and computational models. In *Drainage principles and applications.* II. Theories of Field Drainage and Watershed Runoff. Intnl. Inst. for Rec. and Imp. Publ. No. 16, Vol. II. (The Netherlands).
10. Cronin, L. E. and A. J. Mansueti. 1971. "The Biology of an Estuary." In *A Symposium on the biological significance of estuaries.* Sport Fish. Inst. Washington, D. C.
11. Carter, M. R., L. A. Burns, T. R. Cavinders, K. R. Dugger, P. L. Fore, D. B. Hicks, H. L. Revells and T. W. Schmidt. 1973. Ecosystems analysis of the Big Cypress Swamp and estuary. So. Fla. Ecol. Study, U.S. Environ. Prot. Agency. Naples, Fla. (in press)
12. Clark, J. R. 1967. *Fish and man: conflict in the Atlantic estuaries.* American Littoral Society. Spec. Publ. No. 5.
13. Frankenberg, D., L. R. Pomeroy, L. Bahr, and J. Richardson. 1971. Coastal ecology of recreational development. In *The Georgia Coast: issues and options for recreation.* (C. D. Clement, ed.) The Conservation Foundation and Univ. of Georgia, College of Bus. Adm.
14. Williams, Richard B. 1973. Nutrient levels and phytoplankton productivity in the estuary. In *Proc. Coast. Marsh and Estuary Mgmt. Symp.* (July 17-18, 1972). La. State Univ.
15. Environmental Protection Agency. 1973. Proposed criteria for water quality. Vol. I. U.S. Environ. Prot. Agency. Washington, D. C.
16. Warren, C. E. 1971. *Biology and water pollution control.* W. B. Saunders Co. Philadelphia.
17. Clark, J. R. 1969. "Thermal Pollution and Aquatic Life." *Scientific American,* Vol. 220, No. 3:19-27.
18. Clark, J. R. and W. Brownell. 1973. *Electric power plants in the coastal zone: environmental issues.* American Littoral Society. Spec. Publ. No. 7.
19. Sosin, M. and J. Clark. 1973. *Through the fish's eye.* Harper and Row. New York.
20. Walford, L. A., J. R. Clark and D. G. Devel. 1972. Estuaries. In *Sport Fishing U.S.A.* U.S. Bur. Sport Fish. and Wildlife. Washington, D. C.

21. U.S. Dept. of the Interior. 1968. A study of the disposal of effluent from a large desalinazation plant. Office of Saline Water, R&D Prog. Rept. No. 316.
22. Clark, J. R., and S. E. Smith. 1969. Migratory fish of the Hudson estuary. In *Hudson River Ecology*. New York Dept. of Env. Cons.
23. Chadwick, H. K. 1972. Letter from Calif. Fish and Game Dept. to P. Issakson, N.Y. Publ. Serv. Comm. (Transcript of A.E.C. Licensing Board Hearings on Indian Point Nuclear Plant No. 2.).
24. O'Donnell, J. J. 1972. *Maryland Chesapeake Bay study*. Md. Dept. of State Planning and The Chesapeake Bay Interagency Plann. Comm.
25. Water Resources Council. 1971. Regulation of flood hazard areas. Vol. I, Parts I-IV. U.S. Wat. Res. Council.
26. Atomic Energy Commission. 1972. Guide to the preparation of environmental reports for nuclear power plants. A report "Issued for Comment", U.S. Atomic Energy Commission.
27. Ellis, R. H. 1972. Coastal zone management system: a combination of tools. In *Tools for coastal zone management*. Marine Tech. Soc. Washington, D. C.
28. Governor's Office. 1973. "Bay and Estuarine System Management in the Texas Coastal Zone." In *Project Report Summaries*, Texas Coast. Res. Mgt. Prog., Div. of Planning Coord., Office of the Governor, Austin, Texas.
29. Federal Water Pollution Control Act Amendments of 1972. U.S. Public Law 92-500.
30. NAS-NAE. In press. Water quality criteria. Natl. Academy of Science-Natl. Academy of Engineers.
31. National Technical Advisory Commission. 1968. Water quality criteria. Report to the Secretary of the Interior. Fed. Water Poll. Contr. Admin.
32. Johannes, R. E. Coral Reefs. Unpublished ms.
33. U.S. Geological Survey. 1973. Resource and land information for South Dade County, Florida. U.S. Geo. Survey Invest. I-850. U.S. Dept. of the Interior.
34. Quast, J. C. 1968. Some physical aspects of the inshore environment, particularly as it affects kelpbed fishes. In *Utilization of kelpbed resources in Southern California*. Fish. Bull. No. 139:25-35. Calif. Res. Agency, Dept. of Fish and Game.
35. Fiske, J. D., C. E. Watson, and P. G. Coates. 1966. A study of the marine resources of the North River. Mass. Dept. of Natural Resources, Monograph Ser. No. 3.
36. Smith, F. A., L. Ontolano, R. M. Davis, and R. O. Brush. 1970. Fourteen selected marine resource problems of Long Island, New York: descriptive evaluations. (7722-377) Trav. Res. Corp.
37. Wood, E. J. F., W. E. Odum, and J. C. Zieman. 1969. Influence of sea grasses on the productivity of coastal lagoons. Mem. Simp. Intnl. Lagunas Costeras. UNAM-UNESCO. 1967: 495-502.
38. Roberts, M. F. 1971. *Tidal marshes of Connecticut*. Report Series No. 1. The Connecticut Arboretum. Connecticut College, New London, Conn.
39. Rankin, J. S., Jr. 1961. "Salt Marshes as a Source of Food." In *Connecticut's Coastal Marshes*. The Connecticut Arboretum, Bull. No. 12:8-13. Connecticut College, New London, Conn.
40. Teal, J. M. 1962. "Energy Flow of the Salt Marsh Ecosystem of Georgia." *Ecology*, Vol. 43, No. 4:614-624.
41. Grant, R. R., Jr. and R. Patrick. 1970. Tinicum Marsh as a water purifier. In *Two studies of Tinicum Marsh*. The Conservation Foundation, Washington, D. C.
42. Lugo, A. E. Ecological management of South Florida range ecosystems for maximum environmental quality. Unpublished manuscript.

43. Heald, E. J. and D. C. Tabb. 1973. *Applicability of the interceptor waterway concept to the Rookery Bay area.* Rookery Bay Land Use Studies. Study No. 6. The Conservation Foundation, Washington, D. C.

44. Wass, M. L. and T. D. Wright. 1969. *Coastal wetlands of Virginia.* Spec. Rept. in Applied Mar. Sci. and Ocean Eng. No. 10. Virginia Inst. of Marine Science, Gloucester Point, Va.

45. Savage, T. 1972. *Florida mangroves as shoreline stabilizers.* Fla. Dept. of Nat. Res., Mar. Res. Lab., Prof. Paper Series No. 19.

46. Ragotzie, R. A. 1959. Drainage patterns in salt marshes. *Proceedings, Salt Marsh Conf.,* Marine Institute, Univ. of Georgia.

47. Redfield, A. C. 1959. The Barnstable Marsh. Proceedings, Salt Marsh Conf., Marine Institute, Univ. of Georgia.

48. Dolan, R., B. Hayden, J. Fisher, and P. Godfrey. 1973. *A Strategy for Management of Marine and Lake Systems within the National Park System.* Dune stabilization study. Nat. Sci. Rept. No. 6, National Park Service, U.S. Dept. of the Interior.

49. Currituck County Planning Commission. 1972. The Currituck plan. Outer Banks development potential. Currituck County Planning Commission, North Carolina.

50. Mansueti, R. J. 1961. "Effects of Civilization on Striped Bass and Other Estuarine Biota in Chesapeake Bay and Tributaries." In *Proceedings Gulf and Caribbean Fisheries Institute, 14th Annual Session:* 110-136.

51. Woodwell, G. M., P. H. Rich, and C. A. S. Hall. 1972. Carbon in estuaries. Brookhaven National Laboratory, Public. 17145 (Mimeo).

52. Clark, J. 1969. Testimony before U.S. House of Representatives, Subcommittee on Fish and Wildlife Conservation, Committee on Merchant Marine and Fisheries. June 24, 1969. Ser. No. 91-10:11-26.

53. Clark, J. R. 1968. "Salt-water Fish Prefer Estuaries." *In-Sight,* Bureau of Sport Fisheries and Wildlife, U.S. Dept. of the Interior.

54. Linduska, J. P. (ed.) 1964. *Waterfowl tomorrow.* Bureau of Sport Fisheries and Wildlife. U.S. Dept. of the Interior.

55. Clark, J. R. 1972. Certain effects of once-through cooling systems of Indian Point Units 1 and 2 on Hudson estuary fishes and their environment. Testimony before Atomic Energy Commission Licensing Board.

56. Copeland, B. J., H. T. Odum, and F. N. Mosley. 1974. Migrating subsystems. *Coastal Ecological Systems of the United States,* Volume III. (H. T. Odum, B. J. Copeland and E. A. McMahan, eds.). The Conservation Foundation in cooperation with National Oceanic and Atmospheric Administration.

57. Florida Stat. Ann. §380.012-100 (Supp. 1972).

58. California Pub. Res. Code §2700-27650.

59. U.S. Senate. 1971. Coastal zone management hearings. Subcomm. on Oceans and Atmosphere of Commerce Comm. May 5, 6, and 11, 1971. (Ser. No. 92-15).

60. North Carolina Coastal Zone Management Act of 1973.

61. Florida Coastal Coordinating Council. 1972. *Florida coastal zone management atlas.* Fla. C.C.C. Tallahassee.

62. LaRoe, E. T. 1974. *Environmental considerations for Water Management District No. 6 of Collier County.* Rookery Bay Land Use Studies. Study No. 8. The Conservation Foundation, Washington, D. C.

63. McNulty, J. K., W. N. Lindall, Jr., and J. E. Sykes. 1972. Cooperative Gulf of Mexico estuarine inventory and study. Florida: Phase I, area description. NOAA Tech. Rept. National Marine Fisheries Service Circ.-368. U.S. Dept. of Commerce.

64. Spinner, G. 1969. *Serial atlas of the marine environment. Folio 18: the wildlife, wetlands, and shellfish areas of the Atlantic coastal zone.* American Geographical Society, New York.

65. Newspaper Enterprise Assoc. 1973. *The World Almanac.* Newspaper Enterprise Assoc., New York.

66. Veri, A. R., A. R. Marshall, S. U. Wilson, J. H. Hartwell, *et al.* 1974. *The resource buffer plan: a conceptual land use study.* Rookery Bay land use studies. Study No. 2. The Conservation Foundation, Washington, D. C.

67. Corps of Engineers. 1971. *Shore protection guidelines.* National Shoreline Study. U.S. Army, Corps of Engineers.

68. Code of Federal Regulations. Title 24—Rev. April, 1973. Chapter X—Federal Insurance Administration. Subchapter B—National Flood Insurance Program. §1910.3

69. Corps of Engineers. 1961. Analysis of hurricane problems in coastal areas of Florida. U.S. Army, Corps of Engineers, Jacksonville, Fla.

70. Klein, J., W. J. Schneider, B. F. McPherson and T. J. Buchanan. 1970. Some hydrologic and biologic aspects of the Big Cypress Swamp drainage area, South Florida. Open-File Rept. 70003. U.S. Geol. Survey.

71. Laflen, J. M. and W. C. Moldenhauer. 1971. Soil conservation on agricultural land. J. Soil and Water Cons., Vol. 26, No. 6:225-229.

72. Midwest Res. Inst. 1973. Draft report—Methods for identifying and evaluating the nature and extent of non-point sources of pollutants. EPA Con. No. 68-01-1839. Midwest Res. Inst.

73. Information from F. Ferrigno, N.J. Dept. of Cons. and Economic Development.

74. Clark, W. D., and L. C. Murdock. 1972. *Chester River Study.* Vol. 1. Power plant siting program. Maryland Department of Natural Resources.

75. Bender, W. H. 1971. Soils and septic tanks. Soil Cons. Service, U.S. Dept. of Agriculture. Agr. Info. Bull. No. 349.

76. Born, S. M., and D. A. Yanggen. 1972. Understanding lakes and lake problems. Inland Lake Demonstration Project. University of Wisconsin.

77. American Chemical Society. 1969. *Cleaning our environment, the chemical basis for action.* Am. Chem. Soc.

78. Ketchum, B. H. (ed.). 1972. *The water's edge: critical problems of the coastal zone.* Massachusetts Institute of Technology, Cambridge, Mass.

79. Weinberger, L. W., D. G. Stephan, and F. M. Middleton. 1968. "Solving our Water Problems—Water Renovation and Reuse." *Annals of the New York Academy of Science,* 136, Art. 5, 131.

80. Stevens, R. M. 1972. *Green Land—Clean Streams.* Center for the Study of Federalism, Temple University, Philadelphia, Penn.

81. Veri, A. R. *et al.* 1971. An environmental land planning study for South Dade County, Florida. Center for Urban Studies, University of Miami.

82. California Dept. Pub Works. 1960. Bank and shore protection in California highway practice. Division of Highways, Calif. Dept. of Public Works.

83. Coutant, C. C. 1972. "Evaluating the Ecological Impact of Steam Electric Stations on Aquatic Systems." Paper to Am. Assoc. for the Adv. of Science, Annual Meeting, Washington, D. C.

84. Coutant, C. C. 1971. "Effects on Organisms of Entrainment in Cooling Water. Steps toward Predictability." *Nuclear Safety,* Vol. 12, No. 6:500-607.

85. Atomic Energy Commission. 1972. Final environmental statement—Indian Point No. 2. U.S. Atomic Energy Commission.

86. Letter of Dec. 5, 1973 from Chairman D. L. Ray of the Atomic Energy Commission to U.S. Senator A. Ribicoff.

87. Record of the Maryland Power Plant Siting Act. Vol. 1. State of Maryland.
88. Atomic Energy Commission. 1972. Draft environmental statement—Crystal River Nuclear Station Unit 1. U.S. Atomic Energy Commission.
89. Atomic Energy Commission. 1972. Final environmental statement—Surry Power Station Unit 1. U.S. Atomic Energy Commission.
90. Kolflat, T. D. 1973. "Cooling Towers—State of the Art." Paper given at U.S. Department of the Interior/Atomic Industrial Forum Seminar. Washington, D. C.
91. Burke, Roy III. 1971. A survey of available information describing expected constituents in urban surface runoff; with special emphasis on Gainesville, Florida. Occasional Paper, University of Florida, Dept. of Environmental Engineering.
92. Sartor, J. D. and G. B. Boyd. 1972. *Water pollution aspect of street surface contaminants.* U.S. Environmental Protection Agency, Env. Prot. Tech. Ser. EPA R2-72-081.
93. Thelen, E., W. C. Grover, A. J. Hoiberg, and T. I. Haigh. 1972. "Investigation of Porous Pavements for Urban Runoff Control." U.S. Environmental Protection Agency, Wat. Poll. Contr. Res. Ser., 11034 DUY 03/72.
94. Mallory, C. W. 1973. "The Beneficial Use of Storm Water." U.S. Environmental Protection Agency. Env. Prot. Tech. Ser. EPA R2-73-139.
95. Environmental Protection Agency. 1973. A report on processes, procedures, and methods to control pollution resulting from construction activity (draft). Office of Water Programs, U.S. Environmental Protection Agency.
96. Chapman, V. J. 1960. *Salt Marshes and salt deserts of the world.* New York Interscience Public. Inc.
97. Smith, J. B. 1904. *Report of the New Jersey State Agricultural Experiment Station upon the mosquitoes occurring within the State, their habits and life history, etc.* Macbrellish and Quigley, Trenton, N.J.
98. Bourn, W. S. and C. Cottam. 1950. *Some Biological Effects of Ditching Tidewater Marshes.* Res. Rept. 19. Fish and Wildlife Service, U.S. Department of the Interior.
99. Ferrigno, F., and D. M. Jobbins. 1968. Open marsh water management. *Proc. 55th Ann. Mtg. N.J. Mosq. Exterm. Assn.:* 104-115.
100. Bodola, A. 1970. "An Evaluation of the Effectiveness of Natural Pools, Blind Sumps and Champagne Pools in Reducing Mosquito Production on a Salt Marsh." *Proc. 57 Ann. Mtg. N.J. Mosq. Exterm. Assn.:* 45-56.
101. Ferrigno, F. 1970. "Preliminary Effects of Open Marsh Water Management on the Vegetation and Organisms of the Salt Marsh." Proc. 57th Ann. Mtg. N.J. Mosq. Exterm. Assn.: 79-94.
102. Provost, M. W. (in press). "Salt Marsh Management in Florida." *Proc. Tall Timbers Conf. on Ecological Animal Control by Habitat Management.*
103. Provost, M. W. 1969. "Ecological Control of Salt Marsh Mosquitoes with Side Benefits to Birds. *Proc. Tall Timbers Conf. on Ecological Animal Control by Habitat Management.*
104. Provost, M. W. 1968. "Managing Impounded Salt Marsh for Mosquito Control and Estuarine Resources Conservation." *Proc. Marsh and Est. Mgt. Symp.* Baton Rouge, La. July 19-20, 1967:163-171.
105. U.S. House of Representatives. 1967. *Estuarine areas.* Comm. on Merchant Marine and Fisheries, Report No. 989. 90th Congress, 1st Session.
106. U.S. Dept. of Interior. 1970. National estuary study. Fish and Wildlife Service, Dept. of the Int.
107. Hellier, T. R., and L. S. Kornicker. 1962. Sedimentation from a hydraulic

dredge in a bay. University of Texas, Public. Inst. Mar. Sci., Vol. 8:212-215.

108. LaRoe, E. T. 1973. "Effects of Dredging, Filling and Channelization on Estuarine Resources." Presented at: Fish and Wildlife Values of the Estuarine Environment, A Seminar presented for the Petroleum Industry, by the U.S. Dept. of the Interior, Bur. Sport Fish. and Wildlife. Atlanta, Ga. June 13, 1973.

109. Chapman, C. 1967. "Channelization and Spoiling in Gulf Coast and South Atlantic estuaries." *Proc. Marsh and Est. Mgt. Symp.* Baton Rouge, La. July 19-20, 1967:93-106.

110. Clark, J. R. 1973. The environmental impact of the proposed Seabrook Nuclear Power Plant. Testimony before New Hampshire Bulk Power Supply Site Evaluation Committee. February 8, 1973.

111. Machemehl, J. L. 1971. Engineering Aspects of Waste Disposal in the Estuarine Zone." Conference on Dredge and Fill Legislation, E. Carolina University, Reg. Devel. Inst.

112. Corps of Engineers. 1973. Dredged materials research; miscellaneous paper, D-73-1. U.S. Army, Corps of Engineers.

113. Schlee, J. 1968. "Sand and Gravel on the Continental Shelf off the Northeastern United States." Geological Survey Circular No. 60.

114. Corps of Engineers. 1973. Final E.I.S. Permit Application by Radcliff Materials, Inc. U.S. Army, Corps of Engineers.

115. Goldman, H. B. 1967. *Salt, Sand, and Shells; Mineral Resources of San Francisco Bay.* San Francisco Bay Conservation and Development Commission.

116. Feitler, S. A. 1974. "Mineral Resources of the Coastal Zone." In *Coastal Marsh and Estuary Management* (R. H. Chabreck, ed.): 211-216. La. State Univ., Div. of Cont. Educ.

117. U.S. Dept. of Commerce. 1973. Final E.I.S. Maritime Administration Tanker Construction Program, N.T.I.S. Rept. No. EIS 730725-F: IV-4.

118. Neushul, F. W., and R. Zingmark. 1971. The Santa Barbara oil spill, Part 2: initial effects on intertidal and kelp bed organisms. Env. Poll. Vol. 2:115-134.

119. Kash, D. E., I. L. White, *et al.* 1973. *Energy under the oceans.* A technology assessment of Outer Continental Shelf oil and gas operations. University of Oklahoma Press, Norman, Okla.

120. Wastler, T. A. 1968. "Municipal and Industrial Wastes and the Estuaries of the South Atlantic and Gulf Coasts." In *Proc. Marsh and Est. Mgt. Symp.* Baton Rouge, La. July 19-20, 1967.

121. Calif. State Pollution Control Board. 1954. Report on the investigation of leaching of a sanitary landfill. Public. No. 10.

122. Environmental Protection Agency. 1971. Recommended standards for sanitary landfill design, construction, and evaluation and model sanitary landfill operation agreement. National Solid Waste Management Association and the Federal Solid Waste Management Program. U.S. Environmental Protection Agency.

123. Mannheim, F. T. 1972. Mineral resources off the northeastern coast of the United States. U.S. Geological Survey, Circ. 669.

124. Odum, H. T. 1967. "Biological Circuits and the Marine Systems of Texas." In *Pollution and Marine Ecology.* John Wiley and Sons, Inc. N.Y.

125. O'Neill, T. Q. 1973. Oil Pollution in Long Island Sound. Unpublished thesis. Dartmouth College.

126. Dovel, W. L. 1971. "Fish Eggs and Larvae of the Upper Chesapeake Bay." Spec. Rept. No. 4. University of Maryland, Nat. Res. Inst.